SPECIAL NEEDS

A Daughter's Disability, A Mother's Mission

GAIL FRIZZELL

Gail Frizzell

Published by Gail Frizzell, FrizzellGail@gmail.com

Printed in the United States of America

First Printing, 2018

ISBN: 978-0-578-41402-7

This book is nonfiction and reflects the author's recollections of events. Most names have been changed and dialogue has been recreated.

Visit the author's website at www.GailFrizzell.com

Cover and Interior book design by www.TeaBerryCreative.com

DEDICATION

TO LAUREN

My inspiration and greatest teacher

TO CHERYL, JEAN, JULIE, MARY, NANCY, AND SHERYL

Direct Support Professionals that make Lauren's adult life possible

ACKNOWLEDGEMENTS

Very special thanks must go to my wise and talented friend, Kathy Roberson. Kathy has been my writing mentor for many years. Her encouragement and guidance were critical components of the process and completion of this book. No one could have been more supportive and helpful. Years ago, it was Kathy who taught me that ordinary voices can share extraordinary truths.

Over the last thirty years, many parents have stood beside me in advocacy. They have helped me to learn, grow, and keep moving forward on this long journey. I am exceedingly grateful for the friendships that have carried me through many difficult days. Special thanks to Ellie Byra, who has been my teacher, cheerleader, and great friend since the beginning.

And, thank you to my husband, George. His partnership in caring for Lauren, and his love and concern for her present and future well being, has never wavered.

CONTENTS

INTRODUCTION

When my daughter was born in 1985, my brother's gift to her was a pair of white gloves. He said she was going to need them. He was probably right, at the time.

I was a bit of a perfectionist. Well, truth be told, I was a major perfectionist. It was reflected in every aspect of my very structured life. It was also apparent in my preparation for the birth of my first child. This was something that I planned to do once, and I was determined to be the perfect mother to my one and only child. But the mother I had planned to be was not the mother my child was going to need. A few months after Lauren was born, it became obvious that she was not developing as she should. In fact, I would learn that Lauren had special needs that were going to affect the entire course of her life.

"Special needs" is a term that applies to a broad range of disabilities that start in childhood and will probably persist into adulthood. The disability may relate to a learning issue or may be a mild-to-severe physical, intellectual, behavioral, or mental health issue. My daughter's special needs include severe physical and intellectual challenges.

Over the last 33 years, I have learned that, when raising a child like Lauren, very little goes according to plan. Sharp turns occurred without warning and unknowns piled up like firewood outside our door. Raising this child became a difficult, hands-on, never-ending education in meeting her special needs. It is an education that is essential to share so that meeting the needs of children like Lauren will, hopefully, matter to people other than their own families. This is critically important.

The level of care and length of care required by people like Lauren, who have what is also termed "significant developmental disabilities," is beyond the abilities of most families to provide on their own indefinitely. It is physically and financially exhausting. In addition, many individuals with severe and complex special needs are living longer than ever before due to the wonders of modern medicine. Those adults often have elderly parents, deceased parents, and siblings who have jobs and families of their own in far-flung locations. In other words, after raising these children safely to adulthood, many parents must worry that their children will one day have no one to watch over them or make sure that they're safe and receiving the supports they need.

Despite public recognition of the need for supports such as direct care, housing, and medical care, families continue to deal with inadequate services of sometimes questionable quality and a workforce of underpaid caregivers experiencing unprecedented turnover and vacancy rates. How can they have confidence that their children's tomorrows will be good ones and that anyone will care if they aren't?

Most people have not raised a child with special needs. Many people have never spent time with a person with special needs. I hope that this collection of essays, which spans the years of the life that Lauren and I have shared, will shed some light on the day-to-day lives of individuals with special needs and their families. In particular, these essays will focus on an individual with a degree of special needs that will result in lifelong dependency and substantial daily care requirements.

To have included everything that was noteworthy about the last 33 years would have resulted in volumes, not a single book to tell the tale. Instead, I have chosen to highlight specific issues and subjects that stand out in my mind as representative of the many facets of what now seems like an epic journey that is not yet over. Bear in mind that the issues highlighted here were often not one-time occurrences, but rather representative of ongoing issues and struggles. The essays, read in any order, will tell you about Lauren's life. The essays, read in chronological order, will reveal the unfolding of my own learning and growing experience as the mother of a child with special needs.

Even though Lauren is now 33 years old, our lives are still utterly intertwined. Like a vine winding its tendrils around the trunk of a tree, she depends on my support to survive. But no tree lives forever. In relating the ups and downs, the successes and struggles that Lauren has experienced, I hope that readers will come to know the valiant and worthwhile person inhabiting Lauren's slender frame. Because when I am gone, Lauren will be unable to tell her story or to even speak her own name...let alone ask for what she needs.

For the last three decades, I have advocated for improvement in the system of supports and services on which Lauren, and other individuals with special needs, has no choice but to depend. But the changes are moving forward too slowly, and the funding is not keeping up with need. There are so many urgent matters competing for the attention and compassion of our fellow citizens. How do we compete with terrorism, racism, and political intrigue? The entreaties of the special needs community are not being heard amid the clanging gong of broader, sexier issues.

It is my intention that this book will help people to understand what it takes to raise a child who will be forever dependent and help them to understand the vulnerability of someone who is totally reliant on others for their continued well-being. Perhaps then they will be compelled to add their voices to ours when we speak up for the needs of our loved ones.

This story of Lauren and me is similar to the story of thousands of other mothers and children with significant special needs. Nothing about our lives has been perfect. We tucked any notion of that away early in our children's lives, like Lauren's white gloves now tucked into a drawer and forgotten. We don't need perfect. What we need is to know that our children can live comfortable and safe lives with dignity and with the respect of their communities, whether we can be here to protect them—or not.

AN ENDING AND A BEGINNING

1986—Lauren is six months old

T he stop sign at the hospital parking lot exit was the same as every other—red background, white letters. More than anything else that had been said in the previous two hours, that sign was told me what I needed to know. Much more than a traffic command, it was telling me that my daughter's life, my life, as I had expected it to be, had ended.

We had been shown into a large room poorly lit by fluorescent lights in the high ceiling. I think there were windows, but they must have been curtained, since they did little to eliminate the shadows which lurked in every corner. We were there to meet with an "Early Intervention Team", a group of professionals that would determine if there was something seriously wrong with my baby.

A cherry-red gym mat covered the middle of the tired, gray linoleum floor as if creating a stage for a performance, a place where my beautiful, six-month old daughter would need to perform. I held Lauren in my arms as I sat in a hard, plastic scoop of a chair, the edge of the seat grown roughened from use. Three people that I had never met before introduced themselves with titles that labeled them knowledgeable about child development. They explained each of their roles in testing Lauren to see if she had the appropriate skills for her age. A slim woman with short blond hair took Lauren from me and laid her on the mat. A strong urge to just pick Lauren up and run seized me. We were in an unfamiliar room with unfamiliar people who suddenly had our fate in their hands, and I was terrified.

The woman knelt next to Lauren now lying unfazed on the mat. I noticed that a Winnie-the-Pooh sticker was wedged into the treads of her Nike's, only his head visible, his crinkled body absorbed by the rubber sole. She placed a rattle in Lauren's hand, closing her fingers around both. "Lauren, look the rattle makes noise, shake it, shake it." As she let go, Lauren, uninterested, let the rattle fall to the mat. Moving on she sing songed, "Lau-au-ren," placing her hands over her face. "Lau-au-ren, peek-a-boo!"

Lauren had no reaction. A different toy, a different request, a different game, a different stranger, it made no difference. Lauren showed no interest in anything these people asked of her. Silently, I had been pleading, *Please, please, Lauren, do it, do it.* If she could have heard me would it have made a difference? How could anyone think that my pink and white, sleeps-through-the-night baby was anything less than perfect? I had read all of the books. I had followed all of the rules. What did I do wrong?

The shadowed corners seemed to gather around me as if a curtain was being drawn across a scene I could no longer bear to watch. But I could still hear. The words these strangers were using told me that the suspicions that I thought were just the worries of a new mother were, in fact, reality. My baby was not perfect. She had many, many problems.

Lauren had been born on a steamy, early September night...on my due date. I am a planner, Type A, control freak. A girl, born right on schedule? Perfect! I was so sure that this baby would be a girl. I knew how to do "girl."

Forty-four peach-colored bears stenciled at eye-level marched around the walls of my new baby's room. Each bear held a yellow tulip. Peach and white gingham created a canopy over her crib. My blonde, blue-eyed baby girl would love her fit-for-a-princess room. I was so sure.

Lauren started disproving my expectations from the moment she was born butt first and peed all over the doctor. She has long-lashed, deep brown eyes like her father and soft auburn curls. I think her hair color may be my mother's influence, but I'm not sure what color my mother's natural hair was. During my childhood, "Miss Clairol" paid regular visits to our house.

I vaguely remembered reading that babies who don't turn downward into the usual head-first birthing position may have a problems. But, my brother was born breech, and he was fine.

Preparation for Lauren's arrival had involved doing all of the homework, reading pregnancy and child development books as if I were preparing for a final exam. Once I had passed my part of the test, I was ready to check off each skill achieved and milestone mastered by Lauren. At four months, the boxes that should have been checked were not.

At her next visit with the pediatrician, he asked if I had any concerns, I asked, "Shouldn't Lauren be rolling over by now?"

"Well, yes. Is she holding her head up when she's on her stomach?" he asked, turning Lauren over on the exam table.

"Sometimes."

"Does she reach for toys, grab at things?" he asked.

"No, she's very content."

The doctor played with Lauren, turning her this way and that. Then, without betraying any sense of real alarm, he says, "You could see an Early Intervention Team. They'll test Lauren in a number of developmental areas and be able to tell you if she's delayed...and where to go from there. We'll get you an appointment."

It was not the response I was expecting. I was sure the response would be a placating, "She's fine...All babies are different...She'll do it in her own time." Wouldn't he have noticed himself if there was something wrong? He was the expert. In truth, he didn't seem to be very concerned. Maybe he was just playing it safe, trying to allay a new mother's fears.

Lauren and I had four weeks to "study" before our appointment. We practiced rolling over, holding toys, doing baby pushups. All the while, I prayed, "Let her be okay, let her be okay, please God, let her be okay." She wasn't.

At our meeting with the Early Intervention Team, I had been instructed to make an appointment with a pediatric neurologist. The only thing more terrifying than the imposing title was the fact that it was my baby, my Lauren, who needed to see this doctor.

The neurologist's waiting room was quiet, disrupted only by the ringing phones and muffled voices behind a sliding glass window. A little boy, no more than three years old, sat on his mother's lap rocking back and forth, his dark eyes unfocused, his soft whine wavering as his little body moved to and fro. Another mother lifted a baby out of its carrier on the floor between her and her husband. The baby, whose blue-tinged skin was only slightly paler than his parents, seemed limp, almost boneless, as the mother cradled him in her arms. Were we in the right place? Surely, this was not where we needed to be.

Lauren's name was called and we were shown into an exam room with pale green, concrete block walls and a disturbingly familiar gray linoleum tile floor. The doctor, wiry and expressionless, came in, asked a bunch of questions, and examined Lauren. His all-business approach seemed cold and distant viewed over the head of an infant. I can understand his detachment; he needed to survive spending each day dealing with terrified parents of children with possibly terrifying problems. But, I would have appreciated any glimmer of warmth that could have softened his inevitable conclusion. He told me that Lauren was developmentally delayed and would probably not progress beyond the abilities of a seven-year-old. He spoke quickly, as if the words said rapidly wouldn't sting as much. He had no specific diagnosis. He ordered more testing.

"Do you have any questions?" he asked.

Questions? Framing questions would have required absorbing the enormity of his pronouncement. Asking questions would have necessitated acceptance, understanding, moving beyond the moment when, poised on the brink of the unknown, we had not simply tripped, we had fallen, hard. This was the final verdict. Unrealistically, I had held on to the hope that the Early Intervention Team had been wrong. Perhaps, in the space of the few weeks since we had sat at that stop sign, a miracle had occurred. Some switch in Lauren's tiny head could have been turned on, like the flipping of a circuit breaker. But nothing had changed. The calming words that I had expected to hear had not been uttered; instead, what felt like a death sentence had been pronounced over the soft brown curls of my sweet baby girl.

The questions that I really needed answers to in that moment, when time seemed to have stopped, were *Will I ever breathe again without having to consciously think about it? In, out...in, out? If I try to stand will my legs bear the weight of a heart this heavy?* If I had tried to speak, though, my words would have been swallowed by the sobs I struggled to contain. So, I zipped Lauren's coat, stuffed paperwork about tests and appointments into my purse, and stumbled out of the office.

Back at home, Lauren and I settle into a rocking chair, before I put her down for a nap. The trees outside the window are bare in the March winds, the grass brown, the sky that steely gray of a late afternoon in winter. Holding her warm little body in my arms, I feel that I have irrevocably failed her, that something inadequate in me is sentencing her to a life of misery and want. Tears roll off my cheeks and land on those beautiful curls. Oblivious to my crying, she is content, no less happy than she was that morning. She falls asleep, but I make no move to lie her in her crib. I want to sit here and hold her forever, safe and protected in my arms.

I'm sure I should be thinking about what I will need to do, who I will need to be in order to raise my needful child. But all I can think of is who I am not—not strong or prepared or knowledgeable in any way about the new world in which we have arrived. This was not in my plan. The road beyond that stop sign is not something I can envision. It doesn't even appear to be a road. It is a cliff and the fall is not one that I am sure we will survive.

DESPAIR

1986—Lauren is seven months old

S pring arrives exactly the way it always does. Tiny nubs are unfurling into brilliant green leaves on the maple trees in the backyard. And, the birds have returned. Their calls and trills carried on scented breezes incessantly proclaim an awakening of the earth from the drudgery of winter. But this year, this renewal of life, the return of color, the mingling perfume of blooming flowers, all seem too much to bear. It invites me to join in, to add my own song and spirit to the task of unfolding this new cycle of life. But I can't. I don't want to. I want to be left alone with my grief. I don't want to see the sun. I want to wrap the gray of a long, rainy day around myself and sleep through it all.

There is something wrong with my baby. The pronouncement that came couched in a long term—developmentally delayed, by a stranger with a long title—pediatric neurologist, seemed both simple and unfathomably complex in its revelation, like a spider web upon closer inspection.

There is something seriously, irreversibly, drastically wrong with my baby. How could I not have known? For the last few months, I have held a child in my arms who, suddenly, with the pronouncement of life-altering words, became a changeling, a stranger I had yet to meet. I carried her within me for nine months so sure that I knew who she was and what her future—our future—would be. And, now it's all gone. The hopes and dreams are—poof—never to be realized.

I grieve for the loss of my child, the loss of all that could have been. Not that I don't feel a fierce, protective love for this baby I now hold. But there are two babies in my heart, and I need to grieve for one while searching for a way to move on with the other. Lauren is oblivious, thankfully, to my sorrow. Each day, she requires that I get up, feed her, change her, love her. She is demanding, adorable, and unfazed by other's expectations. She is as content with who she is as I feel lacking in the skills to meet her needs and guilty about the life I have given her. And I feel ashamed because I am bereft that she is not someone else. But there is still a sliver of disbelief poking at me cruelly in a stubborn corner of my brain telling me that this couldn't happen to me, this couldn't happen to my baby. This isn't real. This is just a bad dream. Tomorrow, I will wake to the dazzling green of those new leaves and a flock of chubby robins on the lawn, and I will take my healthy baby outside to introduce her to the sweet fragrance of spring.

But this isn't just a bad dream, and I am struggling to move forward, the fear and despair so intense that I wonder if I should seek escape for both of us. How can I subject my child to a life in which every day will undoubtedly be a struggle? I desperately want to spare her the pain and rejection that I am convinced will become her future. It is my job as her mother to protect her, not subject her to a world unable and unwilling to care for or about her. My only experience with people with developmental disabilities has been others' reactions to them: pitying phrases, intolerance, and exclusion. I cannot envision a future worth living for either of us. If offered the choice of going to sleep with her tiny body in my arms never to wake again, I would gladly make that choice.

But that isn't a choice. Instead, I have to find answers to meeting Lauren's needs. But how do I even frame the questions about something of which I know so little? And when I do, I'm afraid the answers will require more of me than I am capable of giving. I am afraid that, more than anything else, this beautiful child of my creation will deal with my failures forever, my inadequacies persisting in shaping and coloring her life.

Perhaps the only thing I can identify with as trees bloom and birds sing are the tiny tips of plants struggling to push their way through the surface of the hard earth, regardless of what lies above. I understand their struggle to get past the barrier holding them back, but the sun will help them grow and rise above their protected origins. I can't face the sun just yet.

LOWERING A MASK

1986—Lauren is nine months old

Fake it till you make it. It's an approach I've used before, but it only works for so long. It's what I've been doing for months now, putting a brave face on like a mask, hoping, as George Orwell said, that my face would grow to fit it. Behind that mask I was a mess, but to the outside world I was holding it together as a happy, new mom. Most people didn't know, couldn't tell by looking at me or the sweet face of my baby girl that I was anything but happy or that we were dealing with big problems.

I hadn't even told my parents. My mother had been ecstatic to learn that I was expecting. She had assumed, because I hadn't been in any rush to get pregnant after marrying, that I wasn't going to have children. Mom and Dad were living nearby when I delivered Lauren, but left soon after for their winter home in Florida. I kept the doctor visits, testing, and results from them. They had no idea there was anything wrong.

It wasn't to spare them that I kept it from them. It was to spare myself—and Lauren. My parents are good people with simple tastes,

Depression-era babies who worked hard and retired early. They had held on to the norms and beliefs that had served them well as they survived World War II and raised children in the 1960s. But they came from a time when children like Lauren were institutionalized, kept out of sight, and, for all intents and purposes, forgotten. Those poor souls, as my mother would say, that were not "put away" were often ridiculed and marginalized by many in their generation. Well, for that matter, my generation, too.

When I was a little girl, there had been a young man who lived near my grandparents. I can remember sitting in the back seat as we drove down their tree-lined street. The man would be on the sidewalk, walking quickly with an awkward gait. He had ears too big for his head. They stuck out almost like handles too big for a cup. My father would laugh at him. He was called Wahoo. I thought that was actually his name, but now I know it was a nickname someone gave him, not out of love or affection, but out of ridicule.

Even though I was very young, my father's reaction to the young man made me uncomfortable. But I didn't understand that Wahoo had a disability. I don't think my father laughed out of meanness, just igno-rance. It was a common reaction of his generation to someone who didn't fit the norm, someone whose challenges they didn't understand, who more closely resembled a cartoon character to them than their peers. Though this was an early memory, it had stuck with me. There were other memories, too, of discomfort and pity, of whispered remarks when people with special needs had passed through our lives. I couldn't bear for my parents to think about my child in that way.

Perhaps the people who were "different" represented their own worst fears, the fears of dependence, innocence, and nonconformity that would have made surviving in the 1930s and 40s very difficult. It took strength and resilience to rebound from Depression-torn lives and then to weather a world war. Lives of diminished ability, questionable contribution, and in need of care held little value and represented an unfortunate mistake in the fabric of mankind.

I could not bring myself to trust that my parents would love my child unconditionally, that they would not be uncomfortable and distant with a Lauren who didn't "fit in." But they had returned from Florida, and the time had come when I couldn't keep Lauren's issues a secret any longer. It would be obvious very soon that she would not be a typical child, the grandchild they expected.

How do you ease into a conversation like this? How do you tell your parents that you're dealing with a problem so big that even six months after it landed in the middle of your life, you cannot define it, understand its meaning, or the reason it happened? We have no diagnosis, no named evil that has resulted in these developmental delays, a term so vague that it encompasses everything from someone needing extra help learning and, eventually, holding a job, to someone requiring the care equal to that of a newborn for the rest of their lives.

So, I told them what I could. "Lauren is not developing as she should. No one knows why." I continued, "The doctors haven't been able to tell us anything. Lauren's had all kinds of tests, but...we have no answers. All we can do right now is take it day by day."

As if making a pent up confession, I spit it all out quickly. Racing to the end before the threat of tears closed my throat, my short, staccato sentences doing nothing to soften the message. I searched their faces for a reaction. The air was heavy with the possibility of comfort, denial, optimism, contempt. There was only silence. Something in their expressions made me wonder, *did they already know?* Had they been hiding their suspicions from me as much as I was hiding the truth from them? Had they seen through the hollow normalcy that I'd been faking each day since they'd been back from Florida?

The silence wound its emptiness around us, swallowing up the could-have-saids and the should-have-saids. I picked Lauren up and, leaving the room, said, "I need to give Lauren her bath." As I climbed the stairs, I was filled with completely unfounded, righteous anger. I was so angry with them, but for what? They had not been here for me the last few devastating months. But, how could they be? Even if they suspected something was wrong, they couldn't have been sure. They hadn't asked. They hadn't folded me into their arms and offered sympathy or support, not even now. I craved comforting. I wanted them to lie to me and tell me that it was going to be alright.

The reality was that they were probably still trying to process what I'd said. And as for my fear of their lifelong rejection—I was condemning them before they'd uttered a word or even risen off of their chairs.

My anger cooled as Lauren's bath water did. As I put her sleeper on, I actually felt a bit lighter. No more secrets, no more hiding, at least with the people closest to us. My parents' roles as grandparents to Lauren from here on out would be yet another unknown. But there were so many unknowns. This was just one more.

Until their deaths, almost 30 years later, my parents never did say much at all about Lauren's problems. They simply loved her. They accepted her as she was. I came to understand that my reticence in telling them about Lauren's issues that first year was as much about my feeling of failure as it was about my fears that Lauren would be rejected. I thought I had failed to live up to their expectations in some way. What I came to realize was that they didn't expect me to produce the perfect grandchild; they expected me to be best mother I could be to my child. Although my continually reserved parents never said a word to me directly, somehow over those 30 long years, they made me feel that I had not let them down.

EARLY INTERVENTION

1986—Lauren is 12 months old

According to research, the earlier you begin addressing developmental delays in children, the better the outcomes. So just when I'm told the devastating news that my child has a problem and I just want to pull the shades and hide from the reality, I'm expected to seek out and attend a program designed to provide the interventions that my child needs. Of course I'm going to do everything I can to give Lauren the best chance at "catching up," as the term developmental delay seems to imply is possible. But inside the walls of our home, I can evade the truth. It's not pointed out in exquisite detail several times a week just how my child falls short of expectations.

Instead of the Mommy and Me classes and play dates I had anticipated attending with my daughter, we go to an Early Intervention program for children under three that have developmental disabilities. The program is housed in a small, low-slung, brick building that is also a school for older children with disabilities. Crayon drawings and construction paper flowers greet us at the entrance. The receptionist knows us all by name, we mothers of children with big problems gathering in this small lobby. She's a kind, grandmotherly type of person well suited to the role she plays in this place where no one comes by choice.

Soon after we arrive, our children are whisked off to physical therapists, occupational therapists, and speech therapists. A social worker herds the mothers into a small room with several old, brown vinyl couches that emit small poofs of air as each of us sit. This is where sharing our thoughts and concerns as moms of children with special needs is supposed to be uplifting, strengthening, and sustaining, as if our one commonality is enough to bind us. But among the eight of us there are too many differences. We are different ages, some first time mothers, others not. We are different economically, intellectually, and culturally. Forced into this group of unlikely friends by the requirements of the program, we find that our most common issue is our frustration and dissatisfaction with the medical community within which we are all spending an inordinate amount of time.

We have no trouble filling this "support group" meeting with complaints and horror stories about how our children, or we, have been treated by a doctor, a technician, or very often, the billing office of some medical facility. It is a never-ending litany of frustration and despair. But there is no consistently identifiable problem to be addressed. Some doctors are good, nice, compassionate—others are not. Some technicians are gentle, caring, professional—others are not. The only consistent theme is that some people "get it," others do not. And determining whether someone gets it or not often hinges on how well the parent can express themselves, understand their child's issues and needs, or can pay the bill.

There are a lot of tears and monologues of woe in this stuffy room, and the hands on the clock above the door, which is our only escape, move all too slowly. It is consistently painful to listen to the heartbreak of these mothers, of their dashed dreams and unrealistic hopes. One mother has two children in the program, each with different issues. Kaitlyn's heart condition has been getting worse. Amelia, two years older, with completely different issues, is holding her own. Leo, a tiny boy with caramel skin and dark eyes, was adopted from India. He is developmentally delayed, but he is one of the rare bright spots. Leo is making significant progress. He is "catching up", a term we all aspire to apply to our children, as if they are lagging behind in some kind of race. But each week as we watch the Kaitlyns deteriorate and the Leos progress, it is with a peculiar mixture of sadness and envy unparalleled outside of that small room.

When we at last file out through the door, we still have to wait for our children to finish their therapies. I usually wander down the hall and peek through the small window in the door to the therapy room. My daughter has physical therapy last. She hates it, her displeasure voiced loudly and consistently. I want to go in and comfort her, try and help her weather what I'm sure she must feel is an assault. But that is frowned upon. I must trust that the therapists know what they are doing. I am too ill equipped, too inexperienced, to argue the fact. All I can do is watch Lauren cry.

These Early Intervention days are exhausting, physically and emotionally. Lauren will sleep in her car seat on the way home unperturbed by what she seemed to consider abuse a short time ago. As I drive, the comments of the therapists loop in my mind and I search through the tidbits of information shared by a parent or the social worker for something, anything, useful. Lauren is basically healthy, happy, eating well, and sleeping well, but her development is static. Is there something that I could be doing for her that I'm not? How do I research, learn, or give her what she needs when we don't even have a diagnosis?

Soon we are safely back inside the cocoon of our home. Home represents a place where, if I don't think about the doctors and their scary opinions, and I block out what happens in that little brick building, Lauren is simply Lauren, not a child with a problem. Within those walls, she is just my sweet baby girl and I am just a new mom, still a little in awe of the miracle that she represents. I want to try and hold on to that for as long as I can before the cold, hard truth of reality is all that is left.

SEARCHING FOR ANSWERS

1988—Lauren is two years old

f you or a loved one has ever had a medical test ordered to diagnose or rule out a serious illness, you know the anxiety of waiting for the results. The wait itself seems to take on weight and substance preventing you from moving forward, anchoring you in the limbo between panic and relief. And there's not a darn thing you can do about it.

I've been waiting for more than two years now. I'm waiting to find out what is wrong with my baby. The doctors have told me that she isn't normal. "Delayed" is the word they use. But they can't tell me why. Lauren has grown physically right on schedule; she's the right height and weight for her age, but cognitively and developmentally, she is falling farther and farther behind. On a hunch, because that is all that we have left, her pediatric neurologist sent us to see a pediatric ophthalmologist.

At New York University's medical center in New York City, a soft-spoken gray-haired doctor, explained, "We will be doing a procedure called an electroretinogram. Lauren will be sedated. During the procedure we will be measuring the electrical activity in her retinas under different lighting conditions." He assured me that Lauren wouldn't feel anything. He continued, "When we're done in about an hour, someone will come and get you. You can hold Lauren while she comes out of the anesthesia. I'll meet with you afterward to explain my findings. Okay?" The last word was said in an upbeat tone garnished with a small smile that didn't reach his eyes.

I wondered if this was the test, this was the moment in time that I would get a label to place on this threat that was holding my baby, now a toddler that didn't toddle, in its grasp. I wasn't sure I wanted to have a label or a diagnosis whose established history would inform the years ahead. Giving the menace a name would give it permanence; make it impossible to escape its reality in any way. Perhaps it would tear us out of the purgatory we had been in and fling us inescapably into hell.

After about an hour, a nurse returned Lauren to me and she curled up in my arms, still sleepy from the anesthesia. The doctor came into the room and pulled a chair closer to where we sat. "The ERG shows a problem with the rods and cones in Lauren's eyes," he explained. "This indicates that Lauren has a disorder called Leber's Congenital Amaurosis. Leber's is rare and causes vision loss in young children. It is rare that it will cause developmental delays, but it is possible." He concluded with, "I'll send my report to Lauren's neurologist. I'm afraid that at the present time, there is no cure or treatment for this disorder."

There it was, a name for this evil that had been stalking us for the last two years—Leber's Congenital Amaurosis. The doctor had given me some printouts which explained that children with Leber's are usually blind, often have kidney issues, but typically do not have the significant cognitive and physical delays that Lauren has. Since Lauren does not have kidney issues and is not blind, the diagnosis didn't seem to fit. Now I had a name, but was it really the right one? I was doubting the diagnosis and more confused than ever.

The neurologist didn't doubt the diagnosis, but he felt that there was something else going on to cause Lauren's significant issues. He sent us to another doctor, one who had been his teacher at Albert Einstein College of Medicine.

A tall and gauntly thin woman of at least 70, her thinning gray hair bundled into a messy knot at her nape, met us at her office door. She introduced herself as Dr. Meyer and invited us into her tiny office with floor-to-ceiling bookcases along one wall and a paper-strewn desk in the middle. The mingled scents of old books and stale coffee inhabited the room like old friends of its occupant. After taking a seat in front of the desk, I rattled off Lauren's history. "Full term, normal pregnancy, seven pounds, thirteen ounces, Apgar eight/nine. Noticed developmental milestones weren't being achieved at about four months. Subsequently diagnosed at age two and a half with Leber's Congenital Amaurosis by Dr. Barry at NYU. Any subsequent testing as outlined in Dr. Warner's letter has not resulted in a secondary diagnosis."

I had gotten good at this, summing up the last two years of our life in short sentences heavily laden with facts. I had had a lot of practice. Dr. Meyer rose and walked to the bookcases, pulling a large, heavy volume off a shelf almost too high for her to reach. "I'm looking up this disorder, Leber's Congenital Amaurosis," she explained.

The fact that this highly experienced doctor had to look up my daughter's diagnosis scared me. Apparently it was so rare that, in her long career, she had little exposure to it. If it was that rare, could anyone really know the disorder well enough to assign it, without hesitation, as the cause for Lauren's problems?

Besides meeting with this doctor for a consultation, we were also here for Lauren to have a muscle biopsy. Dr. Warner considered it the only test that hadn't been done that could possibly provide another diagnosis. Dr. Meyer explained that she would use a "punch" to extract a small piece of muscle from Lauren's forearm. It would be very quick and require no general anesthesia. I stood to take Lauren into the procedure room and she told me, "Oh no, I'll take her. You can wait here."

I didn't like any of the words—punch, muscle, biopsy. Could I trust this woman? I told her, "I'd prefer to stay with Lauren."

She said, "No, no. We don't allow that." She reached out and took Lauren from me saying over her shoulder, "You can wait here until we're through."

A few minutes later, I heard the gut-wrenching cry of someone who had been attacked and brutally wounded. I knew it was Lauren. I jumped to my feet unsure of what to do, where to go. I had stayed in the room. I hadn't looked to see where she had been taken.

Before I could decide what to do or which direction to run, Dr. Meyer walked back into the room with a whimpering Lauren. The doctor seemed unfazed by inflicting pain on my tiny child. Should a simple test have caused that much pain? Had she used anything to mitigate the pain? Wouldn't my presence, at the very least, have given Lauren comfort? I shouldn't have been so trusting. I should have asked more questions. That's all there ever seemed to be—questions I was afraid to ask, questions I didn't know to ask, questions for which no one seemed to have answers.

Once again, at the end of the long wait for the results of the muscle biopsy, there were no answers. The biopsy revealed nothing. So, I'm finished waiting. I refuse to live in this limbo anymore, as if a label or identity will make any difference in the years ahead. We already know it's a life sentence. At this point, all we can do is go forward one day at a time, which, for me, is almost as difficult as waiting. I want to know what the future holds. I want to get ready. Instead, I will have to let the future reveal itself as it will, because knowing the cause is not going to change its effect. The course of Lauren's life was determined long before she was born.

LEARNING CURVE

1988—Lauren is two years old

There are parenting classes and parenting books, experienced friends and sage family members, all clamoring for the opportunity to inform the steep learning curve of being a new mom. But there is very, very little out there that will teach me how to be a mother to a child with special needs. Trying to figure that out has become an all-consuming task. How do I meet the needs of a child that differs so significantly from others her age?

My little girl is as demanding, and her care as exhausting, as any six month old, except that she is almost three years old. Nearly everything about Lauren seems to be progressing in slow motion. Yet I feel like I'm in a race with her tomorrows, minutes ticking away in which I have not yet found the answers or knowledge that will enable me to help Lauren move forward.

Lauren doesn't walk or feed herself. She's never attempted to utter a word, and there is no way to tell what she actually understands. I should be ending each day worn out from running around after an adventurous tyke instead of tired from carrying Lauren wherever she needs to go. There are no scattered puzzle pieces or balls to toss. Simple baby toys still fill her basket. By now, I should have been chasing imaginary monsters from under the bed and answering a million questions a day; instead, our days continue to be comprised of diaper changes, spoon feeding, and drool bibs.

I am faced with challenges that have no rule book, no Dr. Spock go-to reference for guidance. I want to be everything that Lauren needs in a mother. But, I am constantly questioning myself. What else can I do? What shouldn't I be doing? Did I do something that caused all of this? I long to be checking off the boxes in those developmental charts, the obvious ruler by which Lauren and I will be judged. But what my heart really aches for are the simple mother/child interactions that could soften the edges of the hard truths we are living.

I want to hear Lauren say Mommy. But there is no small, high-pitched voice calling for me, no tiny hand reaching out to grasp mine. Soft little arms never wrap themselves around my neck nor do pink lips plant wet kisses on my cheek. And I don't know if that will ever happen. Perhaps selfishly, I need to know that Lauren loves me, that I mean more to her than for just filling the basic needs of nourishment and physical care.

However, it is becoming increasingly clear that the sweeter rewards of parenthood may escape me. It is as if Lauren's disabilities relegate me to the role of nurse, teacher, and caregiver and steal from me the connection that could heal my heart and feed my soul. And the tomorrows just keep coming with little change and little promise that they will be better.

I can't even turn to friends. They are traveling down different roads with their children. I used to have friends that were on the same trajectory as I was...school, work, marriage, motherhood. But as my mothering experience began to digress from their own, they have drifted away, pulling back from what I guess is, to them, unimaginable. We have so little in common anymore, I guess it's understandable. I realize that I am changing. They may not even recognize me anymore. I am becoming the me that Lauren needs me to be. I can't be the timid girl standing at the back of the crowd like I was for so long. If Lauren isn't going to be able to speak for herself, I'll have to do it for her. There are questions that need to be asked, answers that need to be found. I have a lot of learning to do.

PRESCHOOL

1988—Lauren is three years old

The photos of my daughter's third birthday show a chubby-cheeked little girl in a red T-shirt, a matching red barrette holding her soft, brown curls away from her face. Her long-lashed eyes shine as she looks at the flickering flames of three pink candles in her birthday cheesecake. Lauren had not yet learned to chew so a cheesecake seemed like a good alternative to a traditional birthday cake.

I had planned a little party and invited a few family members to share in the celebration. I was doing what I thought was expected of me. Of course, my little one deserved a birthday party. But, I certainly didn't feel like celebrating. Each of Lauren's birthdays is a marker of sorts, of what has not been achieved, how far she is falling behind. Any hopes that I had that the doctors were wrong, that her delayed development was just that, a delay, a temporary setback, have long since dissolved. Well-meaning people would tell me, "Oh, she'll catch up" or "The doctors don't know everything." But, at three, Lauren was not walking, or even trying to crawl. She never tried to speak, feed herself, or chew. The developmental charts applied to other children, not mine.

This third birthday was about to mark a big change in our lives. Lauren was going to start school. Children with developmental disabilities are entitled by federal law to start school and receive therapies beginning at age three. Unless we experienced a miracle, Lauren would have that entitlement until she turned 21.

On a humid, August morning, I found myself in a cubby hole of a room, barely big enough for a desk and two chairs, at our local school. Before Lauren could begin school, we had to meet with the "Child Study Team". Each school district is responsible for maintaining this team comprised of a school psychologist, a learning disabilities teacher-consultant, and a school social worker. After evaluating your child, the team determines if services are needed and develops a plan to meet the child's needs. I was at the school to meet with a member of the team to discuss their plan for Lauren.

"Well, where do you want her to go?" barked the stocky, middle-aged school psychologist. His shirt sleeves, rolled to the elbow, exposed winter-pale forearms, making me wonder if he had spent the whole summer in that small room. I was at a loss as to why he chose this abrasive demeanor to set the tone for our meeting.

Leaning forward on his paper-strewn desk, he continued, "We don't have anything here for her."

"What do you mean?" I asked.

"We'll send her somewhere." he replied tersely.

"Where?"

"Where do you want her to go?" he repeated.

We were obviously getting nowhere.

"Shouldn't you be telling *me* where Lauren will be going to school?" Frowning, I added, " How would I know where there would be a class to meet her needs?" I was failing miserably at not letting my annoyance show and I really didn't care. I had thought that Lauren would be attending this school. It had never crossed my mind that they would be sending her somewhere else.

"Well, we don't have anything here that can meet Lauren's level of need." he answered. "I guess I can ask around and see what I can find."

He gave the impression that he was doing us some kind of favor, not that this was his job. Wasn't this his job? Wasn't he supposed to already have a plan?

Back in my car, I sat for a few minutes trying to process the last half hour. It was scary enough that this school psychologist was telling me that my daughter's needs were so extensive that they couldn't be met in our local school. But what I couldn't wrap my head around was how little he seemed to care. There was no compassion, no concern, no understanding of the difficult path that we were on. The majority of the professionals we'd dealt with until now—mostly medical—had been kind and compassionate. Now we were dipping our toes in the education arena, and they didn't seem happy that we'd be swimming in their pool.

 The next week, the psychologist called to tell me that the closest program for "multiply handicapped" preschoolers was in a town 30 miles away, across the state border. This was not at all what I was expecting. Apparently, the only option for educating my three-year-old was to send her on a 60-mile daily roundtrip commute on two-lane country roads to another state. But if that *really* was the only option, I guess we had no choice.

Lauren's first day of school required me to come to grips with sending my needy child off to be cared for by strangers that did not know her at all. How could I simply hand Lauren over to them every morning and stay sane until she came home again every afternoon? They wouldn't know just by looking at her or hearing her vocalizations that she was hungry, wet, scared, or tired. If she was a baby, she could communicate those things with a simple cry. If she was a typical three-year-old, she would have words and at least the ability to point. But she was not a baby and she not typical. She was a 30-pound three-year-old with cognitive and physical issues. Her needs were not only more complex, but her communication of those needs perplexing and inscrutable to anyone who had not spent a great deal of time with her.

Going to school was the next step in our lives. Lauren needed more therapy. She needed to spend time with other children. But, I was afraid that she could not survive without me. And how could I survive what my imagination told me was happening to her in my absence?

A 30ish woman driving a tan minivan pulled into our driveway that first school day.

She would be Lauren's "bus driver". In the back of the van were her own two little girls along for the ride. Was this a good idea? In case of an accident, who would she run to first? Or, would she drive more carefully because her own children were on board? She had a perky, dark blonde bob and was chirpily cheerful. Her name was Cathy. I was about to hand over my only child to a complete stranger. Outwardly, I was calm and composed. Inwardly, I was a panicking mess. I struggled to fasten the clips on Lauren's car seat, my fingers rebelling against completing the task. I kissed Lauren goodbye and closed the van door. She was totally unruffled about setting off on a new adventure. I was struggling to hold back tears. Cathy lowered her window and assured me that all would be well, told me what time she'd return, and slowly backed out of the driveway. I turned, walked to my car, got in, and followed the van all the way to school.

The school had taken over the basement of an office building for their classrooms. As each child arrived, school staff would take them out of their car seats and carry them into the building. I watched Lauren being carried in and followed to see where they would take her. Huddled in the classroom doorway, I watched as her sweater was removed and she was settled into a wooden chair arranged in a semi-circle with five others. I was the only mother there. The teacher came over to me, quietly listened to my list of instructions, and assured me that Lauren would be fine. It was time for me to leave. Knowing the right moment would never come; I turned and ran back to my car. I cried all the way home.

At home, the house was eerily quiet. When was the last time I had been in the house alone? I wondered if Lauren was feeling the lack of my presence the way that I felt the absence of hers. Though I had tried to explain, I don't know if she understood what I told her would be happening that day. I wanted her to understand that when she left that morning, she would be coming back home in a few hours. Did she fear that I had abandoned her—scary for her, or did she even care that I wasn't there—devastating for me.

Lauren arrived back home in the afternoon, apparently unfazed by the adventure of her first day of school. I'm not sure if she understood my assurances or not. I'll just have to keep telling her until she does understand that she can always depend on me to protect her and fend off the dragons in her life, whatever form they will take. I have to be sure she knows that I'll always be there for her. That I'll always be there to make her birthday cheesecakes, no matter how many candles light up those pretty brown eyes.

DEPENDENCY

1989—Lauren is four years old

espite the many trees surrounding our house, a robin insists on building a nest in the crook of the drain spout next to our back deck each year. I try to discourage her, but then I get busy and all too soon, the nest is complete and there are blue eggs in it. At that point, I don't have the heart to do anything about it. So, by late spring, I watch as new hatchlings, necks extended, reach for food, fighting with each other to fill their empty bellies. The mother dutifully pushes food into their mouths until she has no more to give, and then flies away to forage for more.

When my daughter was born, I had looked forward to filling her hungry little mouth with special treats, new tastes, and interesting textures. I was going to be as faithful as that mother bird in molding my own little gourmand. I even bought a cookbook containing recipes geared specifically to the tastes of young children. I love to cook and bake, and I hoped that Lauren would share my interest. I could see rainy afternoons when we'd bake together, her little finger swiping the last bit of chocolate cookie dough out of a bowl. Grinning, she'd lick her finger clean. But that never happened. And it never will.

I bake with Lauren, but she just sits nearby, not paying attention to what I'm doing. I hope the smells, the warm kitchen, and our time together is enough, but really, she is missing so much. She's not looking forward to the crumble of warm cookie in her mouth or the taste of melted chocolate on her tongue. I'm not really sure what she understands about our baking project. But we do it anyway.

Lauren's developmental issues mean that she is totally dependent on someone else for all of the food and drink that enters her mouth. My own little baby bird doesn't chew, so all of her food must be soft, whirled in the food processor, or mashed until it's free of lumps and bumps. Sometimes she clamors like one of those winged babies, not wanting to wait one more second for the next spoonful. Frequently, she shows no interest in food. It often takes an hour to get a meal into her. I coax, play airplane, plead, sing songs. I have no idea why she fights eating so much. Sometimes I lose my patience. I sternly reprimand her for being difficult, obstinate, inconsiderate. But she is unfazed, unswayed by my outburst.

Once in awhile, I take Lauren to McDonald's. She seems to enjoy the children's voices, the smells of burgers and fries and the bustle inherent in a fast food restaurant. But I must bring her own food, usually a special "sandwich," pureed fruit, and chocolate pudding. With the exception of ice cream or mashed potatoes, it's rather difficult to find anything Lauren can eat on a restaurant menu. Lauren also loves the food court at the mall. It is a Mecca of voices, colors, sounds, and smells. It's like a party just for her.

Lauren is only four now and I am here to make sure that she has what she needs, but someday I won't be. I can't bear to think of Lauren being hungry and unable to put food in her own mouth, or thirsty and not being able to ask for a drink. The baby robin will one day learn to feed itself. It will grow and fly off well equipped to meet its own needs, find its own way. This is how it's supposed to work, for birds and for children. But Lauren may remain forever like a baby bird dependent on having each morsel prepared and fed to her within the safety of a protective nest.

ADVOCACY

1991—Lauren is six years old

Raising a child with special needs is like being given a job for which you have no experience and have not been educated or trained. But, it's not just a job. Your child's life, now and forevermore, depends on your ability to figure it all out.

When my daughter was in Early Intervention five years ago, I sat with other mothers of children with developmental disabilities. I listened to their sadness, their anger, and watched them cry tears of despair. I had cried, too—buckets. But wallowing is not going to help Lauren. Giving in to the misery that claws at my heart makes this situation about me, and there is no time to make this about me. I have to concentrate on Lauren.

There are a few support groups, but to me, they seem less about support and more about complaining. I cannot move forward with Lauren if I remain within what often seems like a covey of victims. I am desperate for information, desperate to learn about this unfamiliar world I have landed in without a map or tour guide. It has taken a lot of phone calls to make the few good connections that have now brought me to trainings about services, information about education, material on laws, regulations, and rights, and, finally, to advocacy. The other moms that I now meet seem to share my quest. We are training to be warriors for our children.

These moms are voicing opinions and sharing ideas. They are moving past being casualties of circumstance. They find purpose in advocating for the supports their children and families need. They are sharing their strengths with each other, propping each other up when resilience starts to flag. I am in awe of these women. They are teaching me that power lies in our common journey and that support does not mean tear-streaked faces and surrender to the reality of what is without hope for what could be.

These mothers offer me something else, as well: friendship. My old friends have faded away like timeworn photos, their once-crisp images losing their clarity when exposed to the reality of my unrelatable existence. It has been as if we evolved into speaking different languages, mine riddled with terms they don't recognize, and, truthfully, don't want to comprehend. Theirs, holding the ephemera of a parenting experience that I will never know.

Now, I have other women in my life, women with whom I share a common language, a common reality. Meeting them has flipped a switch for me. I have not yet stopped mourning the life that could have been, but I am starting to feel safe prying my fingers away from tightly held dreams that can never come true and reaching for the possibilities of what else might lie ahead. I am not doing this alone. Among these women, I hope to find the strength to embrace reality, not just bemoan it, and to find hope that there may be glimpses of joy to come.

AN UNSEEN ENEMY

1992—Lauren is seven years old

At five a.m., I heard the soft yet staccato rhythm coming from Lauren's room. I threw off the covers and snatched my glasses from the nightstand, as my feet hit the floor. Lauren was having a seizure. I hit the hall light switch as I burst through her door, the light streaming into her room now illuminating her small body at war with the air around her. Her bed was shaking as if its wooden frame was experiencing an earthquake all its own. As suddenly as it began, it ended. Perhaps 60 seconds had gone by. It felt like far longer. Her body continued to jolt every few seconds and then she was quiet. Her eyes began to focus and questions lingered in her gaze. She could not understand what had just happened and I could not explain it to her. How could I possibly explain to her the electrical storm that rages through her brain, racking her body, and leaving her confused and exhausted? She fell back to sleep but I stayed next to her for a while, just listening to her breathe.

Seizures had become an additional hurdle for my already developmentally challenged daughter at 18 months. At first, she only had them when she had a fever, each minor childhood illness carrying an added threat. By the time she was three, they had become a regular part of our lives, and our efforts to find the drugs to control them began. At first we tried phenobarbital. When that wasn't effective enough, Depakene was added but didn't help. Over the course of a few years, we added Diamox, and then terminated it. Dilantin was added next, and that too did not help. Next, we added Depakote, which helped a little, but at this point, Lauren was having 15 to 20 seizures a day.

Often eliminating a medication or adding a new one required a hospital stay and more tests. Some medications affected Lauren's mood making her irritable and lethargic, others affected her appetite, and she would refuse all food. Klonopin caused screaming and even more violent seizures. Each new drug had a strange, foreign-sounding name that I hoped would translate into a remedy for the battle we waged daily. But it was as if we were at war with an unseen enemy, and we were running out of options and ammunition.

Lauren recuperates quickly from a seizure lasting a second or two, but is pale and utterly exhausted if a seizure lasts for a minute or more. Her appetite always suffers on a bad day, and getting her to take her medication, which needs to be taken with food and at four specific times a day, can be an additional battle if she doesn't want to eat.

These seizures, like all of Lauren's challenges, are never something that can be addressed and overcome. Instead of hurdles, they are bricks laid one atop another, a growing and insurmountable barrier between Lauren and the vestiges of normality I had hoped would someday be part of her life. I was devastated when her pediatric neurologist had originally said that Lauren would not progress beyond the developmental age of seven. Now, it is apparent we will never get close to that. I have now reframed that once-devastating pronouncement as an unrealized dream.

More than any of Lauren's many challenges, the seizures claim dominance and control over our lives. And I wonder what the effects all of these seizures are having on her brain. Without warning, they attack. They have control of her, and there is nothing I can do to gain her release. I look at pictures of her when she was younger. There is a light—an awareness in her eyes—that is no longer there. Are these seizures clouding the window through which she sees the world? I wonder if I am slowly losing her with each occurrence, if she is drifting away from me like a child who has waded out into the water beyond the grasp of her mother.

Even after the many seizures that Lauren has endured, the experience never becomes mundane or ordinary. Each one is a battle lost, an event to lament. After each seizure, I have questions that she cannot answer. I wonder what a seizure feels like. Does she have a headache? Does it upset her stomach? Does it make her feel sad, tired, or confused? Sometimes her eyes seem to say, "What was that?" Or I fear they say, "Why did you do that to me?" as if it was I who snuck up on her and caused her harm. After all, mine is the first face she sees afterward.

All I can do is to try to soothe her and hold her trembling frame against me when each assault is over. I speak to her of happy things. She eventually calms and rests quietly. She is unaware of the frustration and grief that my powerlessness etches into my soul. Will the seizures ever calm down, perhaps even disappear as she ages, or will one suddenly take her from me, sweeping her away unexpectedly in one last battle during which her small body finally surrenders?

GRASPING FOR NORMAL

1993—Lauren is eight years old

B
y the time Lauren was eight, our life—Lauren's, her father's, and mine—revolved solely around Lauren's issues and needs. Those issues and needs informed and affected everything that we did. Lauren's seizures, as well as her feeding and mobility challenges, contributed to isolating us as a family and leaving us on the sidelines whenever we attempted to engage in activities and events that most people didn't have to think twice about enjoying.

For example, we took Lauren to our church picnic, spreading our blanket out on the grass with other families. But as those parents and children ran off to enjoy games and mingle, we remained planted on our little island of a blanket, alone. We probably looked standoffish, our lack of engagement unqualified by the challenges of our child. Others were simply enjoying a day with their families, not considering that the isolation of our island was not something we chose.

We didn't venture out to activities often that would highlight the difference between our family and others. Realistically, other parents with children who were Lauren's age were going to soccer games and dance recitals. We had no place there. They were making friends and connections through the activities of their children that we had no opportunity to make. It is the sharing of experiences and similar journeys that give relationships context, and our lives had no correlation with theirs. Being a spectator wasn't enough and, besides, it was too painful to be reminded of our obviously different parenting journey.

However, we needed to figure out something, some way of engaging in life outside of our home. We should be exposing Lauren to the world beyond the carefully cultivated protection of our split-level home in the suburbs. We toyed with the idea of buying a motor home so that we could meet all of Lauren's physical and feeding needs, yet travel wherever we wanted. It would be almost like taking a bit of that protected environment with us. Although, leaving the medical community who knew Lauren and had served her well worried me. When I discussed it with Lauren's neurologist and he said, "Wherever you are, I'm a phone call away. Go!"

So we bought a used motor home and built a secure seat for Lauren right between the two captain's chairs in the front so that she could easily see out of the expansive windshield. The banquette converted into a bed and we added a removable fourth side so that she had a safe place to sleep. A booster seat worked for feeding times. Plenty of storage space allowed us to take diapers, clothing, and all of the food she needed and the small appliances we needed to prepare it. A full-size refrigerator, a bathroom with shower (which was where we stored her wheelchair while on the road), and a generator provided all of the conveniences of home.

Not to say that our camping experience was any more inclusive than our home community experiences. When you open the door of your motor home and carry the pieces of a custom wheelchair outside and reassemble it.....you're noticed. And then when you carry your child outside and strap her into it, your camping neighbors suddenly become very occupied with other activities. Some people would say hello or wave if we were outdoors, but there were no friendly overtures or gatherings on our little campsite.

A trip to Boothbay Harbor, Maine became a regular August destination for us. One year, my husband, George, proposed the idea that we take Lauren on a whale watch. I was not thrilled with the idea. What if Lauren got seasick? What if she didn't like it? If Lauren decided she wanted off the boat, there would be no changing her mind or dissuading her from loudly expressing her displeasure. I'm sure the captain wouldn't turn the boat around just for us, although Lauren might make him wish he could have. In the end, I gave in. Lauren absolutely loved the trip and was a wonderful sailor. I, however, missed the sightings of shiny black seals and elusive whales, since I spent most of the trip hanging over the side of the boat.

Over the years, we have gained confidence in traveling with Lauren. We've made two trips out west from our home on the east coast and two trips to Disney World, where we were welcomed with consideration for Lauren's needs and limitations and all of her favorite music. We have our share of Griswold-worthy stories of mechanical difficulties, bird-size mosquitoes, and quirky campgrounds, but we've never had a problem that was Lauren related. We've had the opportunity to spend chilly, fall evenings around a campfire in Vermont, a carpet of jewel-tone leaves at our feet. We've watched Old Faithful spray steaming water 110 feet high against a startlingly blue Wyoming sky. And, we watched an alligator walk past our campsite in Florida.

All too soon, however, Lauren got too big for me to safely carry her around in the motor home and up and down the narrow-staired entrance. But, I'm glad we traveled when we did and gave her the experiences that were possible in far-flung states. I'm so glad that when I asked that neurologist if we dared to venture out of our self-imposed isolation, he had simply told us "Go!"

And I had listened.

WHEN MOM CAN'T BE MOM

1994—Lauren is nine years old

For many women, becoming a mom means, forevermore, your child is a major priority in your life. Their needs frequently come before your own. Their wants often get fulfilled first. You know that you will probably sacrifice personally to make their lives better. . But when circumstances prevent you from being the mother you want your child to have, it's as if a tangible barrier exists between you and the love you are desperate to express with your care and reveal with your commitment.

The barrier between Lauren and me was represented by the virtual knife lodged in the side of my head, unstinting in its determination to render me unable to function. The migraines had started in my early 20s and worsened after my daughter was born. They would last for a week or more and occurred two or three times a month. The pain would increases in intensity with the slightest head movement, causing nausea and sensitivity to light. If Lauren had been a typical child, it would have been difficult. But, instead, it was impossible.

I would have a window of time to lie in a dark room between when Lauren left for school and when she came home. My husband would be home by seven, hopefully, but he ran his own business and didn't have nine-to-five days.

When Lauren was home, I would need to make her dinner, feed her, toilet her, and give her a bath. Sometimes I could barely stand. Unremitting nausea would have me running to the bathroom worrying about leaving Lauren alone. I would lie on the floor next to the special chair she sat in to be fed and I would reach up to put spoonfuls of food into her mouth. Lauren hated that approach and would get annoyed, refusing to eat.

When George was home, I could retreat to my bed. Sounds from the rest of the house would filter past the closed bedroom door, dishes rattling in the kitchen, the TV droning on with the evening news, and I would stress myself out. George was tired and not very domestic. Did he remember everything I told him? Did Lauren eat? Did she take her pills? She was very picky, difficult to feed at the best of times. There were so many details involved in her care, would she be alright without me?

We had a couple of family members that could sometimes help, but the migraines would affect me for fifteen or more days a month.... you can only ask so much. Reaching out for services from government programs or agencies was unsuccessful. If I had been completely unable to care for Lauren, it would have been one thing, but the sporadic, unpredictable nature of the migraines resulted in our ineligibility for any existing programs.

I had been to specialists in three states. I had a single-spaced, two-column typed page of all the medications that I'd tried. Nothing worked. Even the days without migraine, I'd be exhausted and hungover, an after-effect of the pain. Another headache coming on would feel like a ticking time bomb, the eventual explosion of pain rendering me essentially useless to Lauren. I dreaded calling George, asking him to come home from work. I'd hold off as long as possible and, finally, break down and ask him for help. But he couldn't always come, and the panic of having the critical care of this child in my useless hands would build.

The migraines continued unabated and the stress and fear of potentially risking Lauren's well- being made the situation, and the migraines, worse. The situation also puts stress on our marriage. Both of us were exhausted, just from different reasons.

A friend of George's introduced him to a local woman, Eileen, who had weathered a difficult situation caring for her disabled son by hiring au pairs. I met with Eileen and their current au pair, a young man from Denmark named Jakob. Jakob was friendly and spoke English very well. He had a wonderful relationship with the young man he was providing care for, and was the latest in a series of au pairs that the family had employed successfully.

If we tried this, it would be a financial hardship. But we had no other choice. We were floundering now. How long would it be before we found ourselves in a situation that would become dangerous for Lauren? There were times that the pain got so bad that I literally couldn't move. And George had to work or we wouldn't have a roof over our heads or food on the table. We didn't have another choice to consider, nor time to wait.

Eileen and Jakob guided us through the process and, within a couple of months, Heidi joined our household. Heidi was a burst of joyous energy and enthusiasm in what had become a rather drab and depressing household revolving around problems and pathos. Lauren loved the added attention, and I could feel a little less guilty when a migraine sidelined me. I still felt responsible, though, for letting Lauren down, for not being there whenever and wherever she needs me. I could not change my disabling condition anymore that she could change her's, yet I felt as if I had failed her by not being all that she needed.

Heidi brought laughter back into our home. She was Danish, like Jakob, and loved sharing her culture while learning ours. Her exuberance for life was contagious and helped remove some of the pervasive negativity that we hadn't even realized had grown deep roots within our lives. Having a stranger move into our home was difficult. The loss of privacy required a major adjustment. But, it was a price we had to pay. In the end, the pluses far outnumbered the minuses. Lauren's well- being was secure and she had someone else in her life that had grown to love her.

SPECIAL EDUCATION

1995—Lauren is ten years old

"School days, school days, dear old golden rule days." It's a silly little song from the early 1900s about the innocence of days spent learning "reading, 'riting, and 'rithmetic." Of course, children learn far more than those simple basics now that the world has become more complicated and demanding. Schools also now provide "special education," as if offering an exclusive and important brand of instruction better than "regular education." But it's not, better that is. This is not the kind of "special" to which you look forward or aspire. No, this is the special that means that due to problems with learning, or navigating the world, some children will need specialized instruction, a valiant and worthwhile attempt to close the gap between what should be and what is.

Special education requirements are complicated and governed by both federal and state rules. The rules are meant to preserve the right to an education for all, regardless of abilities. But making rules doesn't guarantee that they are always followed as intended. It's a sad outcome of both the limited resources of school districts and the continuing devaluing by society of individuals who don't measure up to the norm. Investing funding in special education is often questioned by those who think those funds could be better used elsewhere.

I was advised before my daughter entered the special education system that, if I didn't understand the system, know my child's rights, and the school's responsibilities, my child would stand a significant chance of not getting what she needed or what the law assured her. I took that advice seriously.

My Lauren, with her severe delays and challenges, has a window between the ages of 3 and 21 when she can receive the instructions and interventions that will enable her to be whatever she can be. I know that addressing her significant challenges will require far more attention than I alone can provide her. I will need to learn how to make sure the special education services she needs, and is entitled to, are the special education services that she receives.

The extent of Lauren's challenges is becoming clearer as the years of elementary school unfold. At ten, Lauren is still working on holding a block in her hand and learning to walk. Spelling and math are not yet on our list of goals; perhaps they never will be. Lauren is still working on the basics and dependent on others for even the simplest aspects of her life. That dependency is reflected in the art projects she brings home. The colorful paintings are created with an aide's hand guiding her own little hand through sticky paint or, more probably, not touched by Lauren at all since she hates anything done hand over hand. Pity projects, I unkindly call them and never display them on the refrigerator door. They are well intentioned, but sad attempts at portraying normalcy unsupported by reality.

That gap between the compassionate obscuring of Lauren's limitations and actually addressing Lauren's needs is an increasingly contentious issue as the years unfold. Each year, there is an Individualized

Education Plan developed by the team that supports her—teacher, therapists, case manager—which should detail goals and objectives for the year ahead. Instead, often, no goals and objectives of any substance are present, or the ones from the previous year are repeated. I know that Lauren is a tough case, but it is their job to at least try to help her find the keys to unlock her potential, not just give up. Maybe we need to try a different approach, a new angle to helping her achieve and succeed.

If Lauren could learn to communicate with words or some kind of device, she could express herself more clearly in interactions with others. If she could learn to feed herself, operate the joystick of a power wheelchair, or even walk a few steps, she could contribute to her own care. If she could someday learn letters and numbers, maybe she could gain a broader understanding of the world. All of these things could be gateways to a richer and more fulfilling life with less dependency. I have no idea what potential might be locked inside of Lauren, but I still have hope. I often question if other people do.

I push. I coax. I demand that Lauren have goals and that objectives be pursued. I encourage educators to try new things. But will she get what she needs if her education plan is based primarily on my untrained, untested ideas? I have no degree in education, no background in methods or informed approaches to unlocking the potential in a child with severe disabilities. Should I be the one plotting Lauren's course?

I'm not saying that no one in the school cares or that no one has made an effort. We have had some wonderful educators and case managers over the years. Their commitment and choice of career came from a place of generosity and pure desire to help and to make a difference. But their efforts are often hampered by others who are less committed to the goal of special education than to a protection of the bureaucracy that supports it. Taking me aside after one difficult meeting with a team of administrators, teachers, and therapists, an educator told me, "You were right in there. Mary was wrong." I asked why she hadn't spoken up.

She replied, "Oh you know, I have to work with her." It is a sad thing to side with a fellow professional against a child with a disability and her dutiful mother for such a callow reason.

When, year after year, you see your child is falling farther and farther behind, it is hard to stay consistently optimistic, to not fall into at least occasional wells of cynicism. When, at the age of nine or ten, your child has yet to call you Mom or reach out to hold your hand, it is often a challenge to keep pushing forward, seeking answers, being the unrelenting cheerleader that they need you to be. But I'm just not ready to give up on Lauren. Who she is today cannot be all that she can be. She's only ten. Her brain, her muscles, even her bones are still growing and maturing. No one knows what potential any ten-year-old has, why should I expect any different for Lauren?

I certainly understand that hope is difficult to maintain when confronted with such overwhelming needs and challenging impediments. But educators are not entitled to loss of hope. It is their job to pursue potential, to see within each child the hidden possibilities. One of the hardest things to come to terms with is the pessimism that we experience within some educators. Sometimes, expectations and the corresponding effort required are so low for children with serious challenges that job titles could be replaced with "babysitter."

I simply do not have the tools to be teacher, therapist, or learning consultant—and Lauren doesn't have the time for me to learn. I need partners in seeking out Lauren's potential. I need to be able to depend on her school to play its critical role in Lauren's continuing development.

For Lauren and me, "School days, school days…" doesn't hold the same nostalgia or promise of accomplishment sweetly portrayed in that old song. Instead, school days represent the continuing crusade against the challenges that hold Lauren in thrall and ongoing vigilance for resistance to providing the opportunities that just might hold the hope for her tomorrows.

YET ANOTHER CHALLENGE

1996—Lauren is 11 years old

Watching your child with a severe disability interact with peers is both heartwarming and heart-wrenching. It's something you desperately want for them, the joy of having friends, the sharing of childhood. But it also underscores the differences between your child's ability to experience life and other children's. I wonder if my daughter comprehends that her role of observer of the fun is vastly different than the role of participant. I hope she doesn't. Lauren's inability to verbally or physically interact with her peers leaves the ties that bind us to each other unfastened, dangling, and increasingly frayed in their unsecured state. As each year passes and she falls farther behind, the richness and quality of her life becomes narrower than that of the peers that are literally passing her by.

I want desperately to find commonalities that Lauren can share and use to create at least a fragile connection with other children her age. Perhaps if Lauren could at least walk alongside them, meet them at eye level, it would provide a link to that connection. It would be something to add to the plus column now so devoid of entries.

At 11, Lauren is not even attempting to walk. Her ankles are weak, as if lined by rubber rather than bone. Her therapist thought that some type of orthotic or brace would give Lauren the support that she needs and possibly make it easier or more comfortable for her to stand. I made an appointment with a pediatric orthopedist and anticipated walking out with a prescription for the needed solution. I didn't know that this effort to help Lauren walk would reveal a whole new problem and add even more complexity to our search for communal ground.

"Lauren has the beginning of scoliosis, a curvature of her spine, that will probably get worse as she gets older," Dr. Siegel said. "She'll need surgery one day."

I felt slightly dizzy, my brain struggling to keep up with the sudden turn in the conversation. *Wait, wait,* I thought, *we are here about her ankles. Where did this come from?*

"Can't we do anything to prevent the scoliosis from getting worse?" I asked.

"Lauren's scoliosis will have a neurological component," he said. "Most children who have scoliosis don't have that complication. They wear a brace until they stop growing and their bones harden. The brace often successfully halts the progress of the disorder."

"Couldn't Lauren use a brace?" I asked.

"Bracing in Lauren's case wouldn't be effective. When the scoliosis gets to a certain point, we just go in and attach a rod to her spine," he explained, overlooking my reaction to his casually relating that he intended to install a rod in my child's body. "Untreated, the curving of the spine could affect the function of her organs, especially her lungs. Come back in a year and we'll see how she's progressing." He didn't seem to think it was a big deal, but I certainly did.

At Lauren's next visit with her neurologist, we discussed the issue. "Is there really nothing we can do to prevent her from getting worse and needing the surgery?" I asked.

After a beat, he said, "Let's get another opinion. There's a spine specialist in the city. He has an office in the Bronx. Will you go there?"

"Yes," I responded.

After the months-long wait to get an appointment, we found ourselves in an exam room at Dr. Stonefeld's office. A soft-spoken, balding man with courtly old world manners, Dr. Stonefeld examined Lauren, looked at her X-rays, and made notes. He then explained to us that there really hadn't been any studies, nor was there much data available, about scoliosis in children with neurological issues. He thought we should try a brace. "If it doesn't work, surgery is still an option. If it does, you've avoided putting her through a difficult surgery and recuperation." He further explained, "The recuperation time after surgery is lengthy and can be quite uncomfortable. The seizures could also be a complication... during surgery and afterward...when she would need to be very still."

The fact that this doctor saw possibilities, not unproven inevitabilities led me to see just the glimmer of a halo above that balding head. "Okay," I said, "What do we do next?"

"I'm going to send you to my brace maker. She's in Manhattan," he replied.

The brace looked like a medieval torture device. Lauren was encased in heavy white plastic, at least a quarter of an inch thick, from her shoulders to her hips. Inside the brace were bulky leather pads that applied pressure to her spine, pushing it in the direction opposite of the threatening curve. Round leather pads attached to metal bars pushed her shoulders back so that her posture would stay correct. Three Velcro straps tightly bound the contraption to her body while two straps and buckles created a leverage system to keep the shoulder pads in place. I could not imagine how uncomfortable it was. It had to be worn 22 hours a day. How could Lauren sleep in that thing? It was surely going to be insufferable in the summer. How could I possibly force her to wear it, probably for years?

In the beginning, I cried every time I struggled to encase her slim frame in the unyielding plastic, every time I removed it and found the undershirt she wore next to her skin damp and hot, every time I saw the indentations the pads left in her smooth skin. But she did not cry or complain. Lauren did not rebel against wearing the hard and heavy brace. Her grace in tolerating the discomfort and weight was inspiring, yet sad in its quiet acceptance of one more demand on her resilience. I had no right not to match her bravery and stoicism. But the frustrated tears came nonetheless.

Still, in trying to add to Lauren's quality of life by increasing her potential of walking, I had actually failed by decreasing her freedom of movement. It was a good thing we had identified and addressed a problem early, but I couldn't help but think that, in a way, my actions had stolen simple everyday comfort and ease from her life. This scoliosis diagnosis was one more heartbreaking attack on the quality of my sweet girl's life.

Lauren wore the brace for 12 long years. Regular trips to the Bronx and Manhattan were necessary for adjustments, X-rays, and progress checks. In the end, Lauren's scoliosis responded extraordinarily well to the bracing, and she never needed surgery.

CHASING ACCESSIBILITY

1997—Lauren is 12 years old

"The journey of a thousand miles begins with one step." —LaoTzu

"Walk towards the good in life and one day you will arrive." —Atticus

*"The ladder of success is best climbed by stepping
on the rungs of opportunity."* —Rand

For thousands of years, we have used the ability to walk, the ability to propel ourselves through life on two legs, as a metaphor to represent moving forward in the growth toward our potential as human beings. My daughter's *inability* to walk seems like a metaphor as well, representing the many challenges—not just mobility—that prevents her from learning and succeeding in life. She cannot stand or walk or climb. She cannot speak or sign or use a communication device. They are all significant hindrances to Lauren's ability to live a life of value and substance. But one particular challenge, walking, creates a barrier to her even being present in many spaces.

Until now, if we had to go somewhere that was not accessible—an older building, relatives' homes, Christmas tree shopping—we would just carry Lauren. But that doesn't work anymore. She's too heavy. Mobility, for Lauren, means only going somewhere that four wheels can take her. We have persevered in our multilevel home, but as Lauren has reached her preteen years, I can no longer carry her up and down our stairs.

We live in a split-level home with three levels, and there is no way to change its functionality without adding on and there is no room to do that. In order to continue safely caring for Lauren, we have to move. My husband and I considered buying a home and adapting it, but thought it probably easier to just start from scratch. If we are going to make this move, we should prepare for the day when Lauren will be even bigger and heavier. We need to prepare for caring for Lauren physically, as well as allowing her to participate in activities throughout her home. Lauren needs barrier-free entrances and one-floor living with wide doorways and hallways. She needs a roomy bathroom with a roll-in shower so her personal care needs can be safely met.

We are fortunate to be able to make this move. Not all families with similar needs are able to adapt their homes or move to new ones. I know mothers who have to sit their children on steps, inside and outside, and bump them up and down a step at a time. I knew a mother who would place her daughter on a blanket and pull her around the house because a wheelchair couldn't navigate the small and narrow spaces.

It took us 13 months to build our new home. We did as much of the work as we could ourselves. Relatives and friends showed up to lend a hand whenever they could. Lauren's uncle and cousin were there every single weekend. Without their help, it would have taken far longer. It will be a huge relief to move into a space where Lauren is safe, and I am no longer abusing my own body in order to care for hers.

Though we have control over our own home, other spaces are more of a challenge. Prior to the start of middle school in a building new to Lauren, her teacher invited parents to stop in to meet her and see the classroom assigned to children with multiple disabilities. This school had served our community for more than 50 years, first as a high school and now as a middle school. I knew we were in trouble the moment I saw where the classroom was located. I knew the layout of the building since I had attended there for three years myself 30 years ago. The classroom, the cafeteria, the nurse's office, the auditorium, the gym, and the main office were all on different levels as a result of multiple remodels done many years ago. That meant multiple staircases with no elevators or ramps. A classroom near the only entrance accessible to the parking lot had been selected for Lauren's class. It just wasn't accessible to anything else inside the school.

I asked Lauren's new teacher, "How will Lauren get to the cafeteria?"

She replied, "Oh, we thought we'd have lunch in the classroom."

Excusing myself, I headed for the principal's office. It was still near the front entrance, exactly where it had been when I attended school there. Unfortunately for him, he was in his office and the door was open.

After introducing myself, I outlined the lack of accommodation made for Lauren and her classmates, several of whom also used wheelchairs. This school had not yet served students with severe physical disabilities, and they had definitely not thought the challenge through or considered their responsibilities by law. Apparently, the administration had planned to simply corral these new students in the back of the building, like the more dangerous animals in the zoo. I explained to the principal that Lauren would be attending programs in the auditorium with the rest of the school, that she loved lunch in the cafeteria, and that an adapted gym program would need to be provided. I could see the reaction in his eyes, *Oh crap, she's one of those parents.*

The principal went into problem solving mode fairly quickly and called me a few days later to confidently explain that Lauren's class could use a back door near their room to access an exterior courtyard, which they could then cross to use an already ramped exterior entrance to the cafeteria.

"In the middle of the winter ... in the rain?" I asked.

"Well, yes," he replied. "It's an old building. It's the only option we have." He continued, "Why don't you come back in and we'll walk through our options."

The next afternoon I met the principal at his office and then followed him down the hall to the cafeteria. We stopped in front of the door that he had mentioned was the ramped courtyard entrance. In getting ready for the new school year, maintenance staff had installed a shiny new freezer that very morning...in front of the rarely used courtyard door.

The principal, now a deep shade of pink, said "I'll take care of this immediately."

The doorway was ready for use by the time school started. It was definitely not an ideal solution, but I had learned to pick my battles. Without major renovations, this was the best alternative. It was more important for Lauren to be in this school, with her peers, than to be sent somewhere else while those renovations were made, a process that would probably take at least a year or two. If sent elsewhere, she would lose the tenuous connection that she had with her peers, typical and not, that she had been in school with since kindergarten. Exposure to some inclement weather was worth preserving the familiarity she had with at least a few people her own age.

Although school and home are probably the major destinations for Lauren right now, there is a big world beyond the protected walls of those buildings. Accessibility has become an added challenge in her life and has the potential to profoundly increase her isolation from mainstream life. Even though there are laws about accessibility in new construction, much of our world is not new and, therefore, much of our world is inaccessible.

Lauren's world is already narrower because of her disabilities. I need to make sure that, although she cannot *step* into her future, she can *roll* into as much of it as possible.

INCLUSION

1999—Lauren is 14 years old

The high school years are a critical time for teens to explore who they are, develop talents and interests, and grow emotionally, socially, and spiritually. It's an intense few years on many levels, and there is an unmistakable momentum toward adulthood, toward the freedoms and responsibilities of their futures.

For teens with severe disabilities, it is a time when the disparity between their development and that of their typical peers becomes especially apparent. But it is also a time when relationships formed between typical students and those with severe disabilities can become building blocks for the future. These building blocks are critical in the forming of attitudes of acceptance that can be carried into adult interactions.

Advocacy had been necessary to ensure Lauren was included in elementary school classes with her typically developing peers. But the school had been open to creating opportunities for both regular and special education students to learn from each other. In high school, however, we were encountering stiff resistance to our attempts at inclusion beyond eating lunch at a segregated table in the cafeteria. In elementary school, children with special needs were accepted as part of the school body; different, but still "family.". In high school, it was as if they were unwanted neighbors with a culture and lifestyle too disparate to warrant interaction.

I didn't want inclusion experiences to end. They were too important for both Lauren and her regular education peers. Lauren needed to be accepted, and respected, as part of the student body—the same group of individuals who would need to accept her when they all became adults. But, did I want to push Lauren into a situation where she was so obviously not welcome? I didn't expect that Lauren would be included in serious lecture-based classes, such as history or algebra. I didn't ask for her to participate in a class where her inability to conform would be disruptive to other students. A less structured class, such as home economics or art would be better, where there was more activity and interaction with peers. The administration let me know very clearly that they didn't like it, but would comply because special education law didn't give them a choice.

On Back to School night of Lauren's freshman year, I spent some time in her multiply handicapped classroom, located in the nether reaches of the school near the wood shop. When the schedule rotated to Lauren's third period cooking class, I filed into the class with the other parents and listened to the teacher, Mrs. Pierce, explain her plan for the year. At the end of her speech, she told us that there was a student with special needs in the class that year. "But, you shouldn't be concerned," she assured us. She then proceeded to explain the nature of Lauren's disabilities in detail. She continued, "This student is in this class for socialization. Sometimes, children with special needs are allowed in regular classrooms."

In this short speech, she had broken all of the confidentiality rules, classified my child as an inferior member of the class, and disavowed any responsibility to oversee the goals and objectives in Lauren's education plan. She was worried that the parents of the other children would be concerned that Lauren would be in the same classroom as their children. I did not know what that meant. Lauren uses a wheelchair that she cannot propel herself and doesn't speak. How could Lauren represent any kind of threat?

I didn't trust myself, at that moment, to explain to this teacher in a constructive manner what she had done wrong. I filed out of the classroom with the other parents, stopping at the classroom door to introduce myself before leaving. I wanted Mrs. Pierce to know that I had been there.

Still distressed by the experience the next day, I wrote Mrs. Pierce a letter explaining how her speech the night before was not just inappropriate but illegal. In addition, I wrote:

> "You explained Lauren's presence in your class to the other parents as an anomaly, a concession, not that she has as much right as their own children to be there. If Lauren is ever going to be valued as a member of her community as an adult, it must begin now. She will never find acceptance if myths and prejudices are perpetuated. In your classroom Thursday night there were ten people who had those myths and prejudices reinforced for them by a teacher, a respected member of the community, someone who needs to set an example."

She replied with a written apology simply stating that she meant no harm, but seemingly not grasping the significance of her words or her dismissal of Lauren's rightful place among her classmates.

Unfortunately, school was not the only place where Lauren's right to simply be present, to be recognized as a rightful participant, was a problem. We had been attending Sunday Mass as a family since Lauren was born. Lauren loved the music most of all, humming along with the choir, often continuing to hum long after each hymn was over. No one seemed to mind.

The pastor of the church we had been attending for several years was welcoming and attentive. It was he who had taken the initiative to pull me into his office and say, "Let's have Lauren make her First Communion and her Confirmation." I had thought Lauren's cognitive issues would render her ineligible to receive these particular sacraments of her church. I had saved my own First Communion outfit to hand down to a daughter one day. But when other little girls her age were wearing their frilly white dresses, including Lauren did not seem possible. I had pushed the dress to the back of the closet. Now that Lauren was a little older, Father Brien told me we would find a way to include Lauren in the grace represented by these sacraments.

I worked with Father Brien to adjust expectations for a child who doesn't chew (no bread) and who would need the sacrament preparation pared down to her cognitive abilities. He created a First Communion ceremony at a Sunday Mass just for Lauren. She couldn't wear the dress, but she did wear the tiny wreath of silk flowers in her dark curls that I had worn at my First Communion. The entire congregation roared with applause as I turned from the altar to wheel Lauren back to our pew. I had thought this day would never happen, and I was grateful for the love and acceptance that our fellow parishioners were showing.

Two years later, Lauren made her Confirmation along with other teens in a formal ceremony presided over by our bishop resplendent in his red robes. This time, it was the bishop who took me aside and said, "I'm so glad you did this for her."

After the warm acceptance Lauren had received, I was unprepared for what happened when a new pastor joined our church. When we introduced ourselves to Father Stephen on our way into church one Sunday, I explained how the previous pastor and I had worked out communion for Lauren (Lauren couldn't chew, so no host). He said, "You can wait for me after Mass, and I'll give Lauren communion then so that she won't disturb anyone."

It took me a minute to absorb what he had said. I then explained, "Lauren has been receiving communion with her parish community since her First Communion. She's not disturbing anyone." More parishioners were starting to arrive and this had suddenly become a much more important conversation than we could have at that moment. "I'll be in touch with you this week," I said. "We need to discuss this further."

He looked a little surprised, and turned away, moving on to other parishioners.

Our short conversation had pushed so many buttons for me that I wasn't even sure how to begin to explain to a priest the ideas of acceptance, inclusion, and community. I decided that, again, I would write a letter. I didn't want to antagonize the man, and I didn't trust myself to stifle my anger in a face-to-face meeting. Putting my thoughts down on paper would give me an opportunity to vent...and then delete—an option sorely needed in human interactions.

My letter to Father Stephen said...

After our recent conversation, I feel that you may not fully understand Lauren's role in her parish community and in the world in general. Since Lauren was a baby I have had to fight to keep her from being segregated, isolated, and excluded in her community and in her school. The one place where she was always accepted and welcomed was in her church. A few years ago she made her First Communion in front of, and with the encouragement of, her assembled fellow parishioners at a 9:30 mass. Two years later, after finishing preparation for Confirmation with her peers, she made her Confirmation at the parish celebration of the sacrament. She did so with the enthusiastic support of Bishop Ratimer.

On a daily basis Lauren has to face the challenge of people being so blinded by her disabilities that they fail to see her many gifts, among them strength, integrity, and enthusiasm for her simple life. It takes time to get to know and understand Lauren. Because she does not communicate in a socially-prescribed manner, people think she does not understand what is going on around her. When you get to know Lauren and can read her expressions and mannerisms, you come to realize that Lauren absorbs much of what she sees and hears, and that she definitely has opinions and thoughts of her own. Do not underestimate her. She is a teacher of many things including the fact that everyone has value and a place in their community. Through Lauren people will learn joy is present in all of us and that we all have gifts to contribute. But, she cannot teach unless she participates in the mainstream of her community.

I am rather taken aback that at this time you would seek to exclude Lauren from participating in Communion along with her parish community. She has been receiving Communion as part of Mass since her First Communion. There has never been a question of her disturbing her fellow parishioners or of due reverence not being given the sacrament. I would like Lauren to continue receiving communion during mass along with her fellow parishioners. I do not feel it necessary or appropriate for Lauren to receive communion after mass.

The next Sunday, Father Stephen greeted us by saying, "I received your letter. There will be no problem with Lauren receiving communion during the Mass."

That connection—time spent sharing minutes and hours with other people—is where understanding and caring are born. It is critical for a young woman lacking normal communication skills to have that time to develop ties with peers and parishioners, community members and community leaders. It is during that time that the people who will inhabit

Lauren's tomorrows will develop the empathy and respect that are critical to her ongoing quality of life and safety.

We are battling long-held beliefs, fears, and misunderstandings. But, it shouldn't be a battle to be included, to avoid being set aside as dangerous or disturbing simply because your abilities are different than the norm. That said, I wonder how I would react to a "Lauren" passing through my life if I did not have the experience of raising her. Honestly, I can see myself being unsure of how she could fit into my world, of avoiding being caught out in my ignorance. So I understand when we face resistance that it doesn't help to get angry. It is more important to make sure that Lauren is given the opportunity to teach and to help people change their understanding of people with developmental disabilities. I can speak from experience that Lauren is the best teacher that they could have.

As it turned out, Father Stephen was only with our parish for a short time. Seven or eight years after he left, I ran into him at a local restaurant. The first question he asked was, "How is Lauren?" After all of those years, and the many people that had probably filtered through his life, he had not forgotten the girl in the pink wheelchair who sometimes continued "singing" after the choir had finished. She had been a memorable member of a parish he had served.

BROKEN THREADS

2001—Lauren is 16 years old

f you Google "effects of having a child with special needs on a marriage," your search will reveal a slew of studies and articles on the frequency of divorce. The oft-reported statistic was an 80% divorce rate in marriages with a child with a disability. More recent studies seem to have disproven that number, showing only a slight increase over the norm.

Rather than focusing on the divorce rate, I think it would be more compelling to look at the quality of marriages between couples raising a child with special needs and those who are not. Does the happiness or satisfaction in the marriage significantly differ compared to parents who are not raising a child with special needs?

I know quite a few couples that stayed together, not because the marriage was working, but rather because other factors prevented the option of divorce. If the mother stopped working to take care of the disabled child, or the care restricted her career in any way, she may not be able to afford to raise the child on her own. That "child" could now be

a teenager or adult, representing many years out of mainstream employment. Even if there is financial stability, supporting two households and
the costs associated with meeting the child's needs may be prohibitive.
Possibly, the care level of the child may be so extensive that one parent
cannot handle it on their own. Or, the process of divorcing and building
new lives is more than either parent can consider on top of their already
overburdened lives. So they stay married. They may be unhappy. They
may be miserable. But they don't see the alternative as supportable. They
may also fear being alone forever. As one mother I know put it, "Who
would take me on with this much baggage?"

Over the years of raising my own child with severe disabilities, I've
become friends with many other moms on the same journey. Although
our children share a great deal of the same needs, and the requirements
of caring for them are somewhat similar, our marriages are vastly
different. Among us, there are beautiful marriages, good partnerships,
floundering relationships, marriages of convenience, and divorces. The
level of need of the child does not seem to universally affect the quality
of the marriage. What does seem prevalent is the inability of unhappy
partners to do anything about their discontent. These marriages may
have deteriorated even without the presence of a child with special needs.
But because of the extensive needs of a son or daughter, staying together
has been a necessity rather than a choice.

I worry about my own marriage. We were once a couple who lamented
each moment apart, who never played music in the car because we were
too busy talking, planning, dreaming. We worked together, we played
together, and then we added another beautiful facet to our world—a
child. That child needed such focus, so much time and attention, that
we poured all that we had into meeting her needs, leaving little for each
other. We divide and conquer our responsibilities now, our conversations
devoted to catching each other up on our progress. George is running a
business and pitching in when he can with Lauren. I run the business of

Lauren—school, therapy, doctors, and the care and feeding of a 16-year-old who does not walk or talk or feed herself.

Maybe it's typical to get overwhelmed with the needs of children, to lose sight of each other in the mayhem. But that busyness usually ends, kids grow up, become at least marginally independent and, hopefully, build lives of their own. That will never happen with Lauren. She will need an intense level of care for her entire life. Perhaps George and I have lost each other forever, too tired to reclaim what once was. This journey may have changed us so thoroughly that, one day, we may not be able to remember the "we" that used to be. Like stones smoothed by a crashing sea, we will appear changed, our surfaces weathered and eroded. And what then? Lauren will still need both of us. Neither of us will have the freedom to simply walk away, to revisit old dreams or seek out new ones.

The stress and fatigue of day-to-day care and the frustrations linked to navigating service systems, advocating for education, dealing with medical issues, and the like cannot help but build until something gives. I get tired of being reasonable and rational. Sometimes I just need someone to blame…for something. Most days, the only person I see besides Lauren is my husband. His freedom to come and go seemingly as he pleases rankles me. Each day, he goes off to deal with other people's needs, and I am stuck at home dealing with old and new challenges that I can never walk away from, can never get on top of, and can never choose to ignore.

I know George needs to run a business, make a living, and prepare to support our child, probably forever. He can't let Lauren's needs take over his every waking moment. I know I'm not being fair. Where on Earth would we be if George did not provide so well for all of us? But some days, by the time he comes home at six or seven, my nerves are frayed, and he is a convenient dartboard for the arrows of angst that I've been hoarding all day.

George, on the other hand, tends to keep things bottled up. He doesn't share how he's feeling. He doesn't call me on my unnecessary criticisms, and he interprets my complaints as problems he must solve, not just my need to vent. Overall, it's not a recipe for domestic bliss.

What is the factor that allows some marriages to weather the storms and strains of raising a child with special needs better than others? Would the unhappy ones have become unhappy anyway, an illness, a financial setback, an impasse tipping them over the edge? Is it the needs of the child that rend the fabric of the marriage? Or, is the warp and weft of the marriage wanting, too weak to weather the battle wounds and pummeling crises that leave it threadbare?

Whatever the reason, whatever the cause, it seems that, for some of us, the continuing care of a child with special needs is sometimes the last unbreakable thread that binds two parents together. It is the one thread that we won't allow to be broken.

RITES OF PASSAGE

2003—Lauren is 17 years old

E ven though special education law, which ensures the rights of all children to receive a free and appropriate education has been around since 1975, there remains pockets of reluctance to support the right of students with developmental disabilities to be present and welcomed in their schools. This disinclination has been prevalent and persistent throughout my daughter's high school years, much more than her elementary school years. Perhaps the intensified focus on preparing students to meet the requirements of adult lives seems futile when applied to students perceived as having little chance of achieving independent lives. It often feels like there is a defined space that special education students are supposed to remain within. Creativity or efforts to span the divide of special and regular education, therefore, are often met with resistance and downright annoyance.

It can be daunting for a parent to face that resistance and push past the barriers it represents. Like a fence we can see through but still stands in our way, it takes diplomacy and diligence to wiggle our way through to assure that our children have not only the educational experiences that they need, but the extracurricular ones, as well.

I wanted to make sure that Lauren experienced everything that high school could offer her, even if it was far less than most students experienced. Getting educators to make an effort to include Lauren in the informal education opportunities that comprise a more complete educational experience had been difficult. Students like Lauren often miss out on the social and extracurricular activities that are a huge part of the high school years. Lauren's school has made some effort to bring regular education students into the special education classroom on a regular basis and to have students like Lauren attend the dress rehearsals of the school plays and concerts. But those efforts were still limiting the special education students to a very narrow exposure to the student body and school experiences.

During Lauren's senior year, I realized that she would be missing out on one of the major rites of passage of high school: the prom. When I approached Lauren's teacher with the request that Lauren attend the prom, she said, "Well, we've never done that before." Since the prom was a school function, the school couldn't legally prevent Lauren from attending. And they would only need to make some simple changes to accommodate Lauren.

When a few other parents learned that Lauren was going to the prom, they also requested that their children with special needs attend. The school made the necessary accommodations, arranging for special education aides to attend with the prom-going students. They also put out a request for volunteer escorts among the regular education students. So many students volunteered that they had to turn some away. For the first time in the school's history, special education students would be included in one of the most important extracurricular events of the school year.

Lauren has missed out on a lot of the non-educational aspects of school and childhood...and so have I. There have been no dance classes or soccer games, Girl Scouts or gymnastics. Lauren and I have not had those average childhood moments that leave wonderful memories in their wake. So, for this girly-girl mom, the prom wasn't just about Lauren attending a dance, it was also about the preparations for the prom that we could share. First, there was the prom dress shopping. We had to find something that would work with the wheelchair and that Lauren would be comfortable in. It wasn't practical for Lauren to try on multiple dresses, nor would she tolerate the process. Fortunately, we are the same size, so I tried them on and narrowed it down to two. Together, we selected the perfect dress: pale pink satin with a beaded bodice and secure straps.

In her beautiful dress with tiny pink flowers peeking out from the shining curls I had gathered at her crown, Lauren sat regally on a living room chair while I snapped photos. Her usual rocking movement stilled as if she grasped the importance of this special evening. A few family members stopped by to ooh and aah over a stunning Lauren. Pretty in pink. For the first time, we were seeing beyond the childlike demeanor and frame that made strangers think that Lauren was much younger. On prom night, we saw a 17-year-old on the brink of adulthood.

At the venue, Lauren was met by the tall, strapping football player who had volunteered to be her escort. Seven other young men and women with special needs all dressed in prom finery joined them with their own escorts. I was surprised to be greeted by name by a few of the escorts. Then I realized these grown-up looking young men and women had been in an elementary school class with Lauren, in which a regular education teacher was particularly enthusiastic about the benefits of inclusion.

When my husband and I returned hours later to pick Lauren up, we were met by Lauren's aide, Sandy, who had been watching over her throughout the evening. "You have to see this," she said, "Come on."

We followed her into the ballroom vibrating with the bodies of 200 teenagers dancing to "YMCA" under sparkling lights. Sandy pointed to the middle of the dance floor. Lauren's wheelchair moved to the beat surrounded by other happy-faced prom-goers. Lauren was glowing, oblivious to our presence, and embodying the exuberance of those surrounding her. She had spent a rare night not on the sidelines, but included.

Although I resolutely fought for Lauren's inclusion throughout her school years, I sometimes wondered if it mattered to Lauren. She could never tell me. But I think my answer was in the radiance of prom night, which stayed with Lauren for days afterward. In her own way, she was telling me...*You did good, Mom.*

Our next challenges centered on graduation. Lauren, as a special education student, was entitled to receive services until she was 21. However, I requested that she participate in her senior-year graduation ceremony, at 17, with the peers she had attended school with since she was five years old.

When I was told that I would need to meet with the superintendent of schools, I knew this meeting was not going to go well. Any other requests that I had made over the years had been handled by lower level staff, but I hadn't accepted "no" from the teacher, the case manager, or the principal on this issue, and they were pulling out the big guns.

This request for Lauren to participate in graduation was a bit of a gray area since she was not technically graduating. However, the ceremony would have meaning to Lauren shared with familiar peers now. It would have little in three years shared with strangers three or four years younger than her. Other schools were recognizing the importance of the timing of this milestone, and it was becoming common practice to allow students with special needs to participate in graduation their senior year. Many of the students with special needs would never meet the mandated graduation requirements for high school, so, for them, graduation was a celebration of completing 12 years of school with peers. It represented a turning point in their education toward a transition to adult lives. The pomp and circumstance of the day, at the typical age, with their typical peers, had more value in their lives than it ever would if it occurred simply because they had aged out of federally mandated schooling.

However, the superintendent was adamant at our meeting. "No. It would not be appropriate," he insisted. "Technically, Lauren is not graduating. She'll be with us for a few more years."

My husband had joined me at this meeting. He usually let me be the education advocate, content to cheer from the sidelines. But I had met so much resistance with this request that he thought he needed to be there, at least for moral support.

I had prepared myself for opposition. "School districts across the country are recognizing the importance of meeting not only educational goals but social ones, and they allow students in special education to participate in graduation ceremonies," I reasoned.

"Well, we don't do that here," the superintendent said dismissively.

"Why?" I asked.

"It wouldn't be fair to the other students who have completed the graduation requirements."

"If that's the criteria for participating in the graduation ceremony, Lauren will never be able to participate," I pointed out.

"We won't be changing our policy for Lauren. I'm sorry, I have another meeting," he replied. Then he stood and walked around his desk to usher us out of his office.

George had been letting me do the talking. His heel, tapping at an increasingly rapid rate was telegraphing his irritation loud and clear. At the last dismissive pronouncement, George leaned forward, about to interject a comment that I knew could only intensify the growing tension in the office. I stood, tugging on George's arm, turned and left the office. The superintendent may have thought the issue was concluded. I knew it wasn't.

I wasn't asking for Lauren to do more than participate in a ceremony with the same classmates that she had contact with for 12 years. She may not know them well, but I hope that they knew her. They would all soon be leaving. In a few years when Lauren left school for good, she would have no history, no long-term familiarity with the other students graduating at that time. They would be strangers. It was important to mark the transition from childhood to young adulthood with ritual, with celebration, and with fellow travelers. There was nothing in education law that prohibited Lauren from putting on a cap and gown with the class of 2004. And I was determined to make it happen.

I immediately rallied support. The superintendent of a neighboring school district was a friend, I called him and he promised to contact our superintendent and express his support of our request. I called the State Division of Special Education, told them what was going on, and they promised to write a letter. Other advocates, eager to support us, wrote letters, as well.

About three weeks after our initial meeting, a letter arrived from the superintendent. In it he announced that Lauren would be allowed to participate in the graduation ceremony against the advice of the district. He berated us, as her parents, for "putting her health and well-being at risk" by making this request for Lauren to participate in a ceremony in June when the weather *could* be hot. Apparently, the only point he could find to take a stand on was the fact that he didn't believe we would have the sense to make whatever adjustments the weather demanded when that day arrived.

Graduation morning arrived sunny and pleasant, a cool breeze sending the gowns of graduates billowing like red and silver flags. Lauren and her aide took their places in the line of other students as they marched onto the field. When Lauren's name was called, the aide wheeled her to the podium where a red leatherette folder was placed on her lap. Back in her place among the other seated graduates, it was hard to pick her out, the mortarboard on her head blending into the sea of other red and silver squares.

It took a campaign to get us through this "no" and, after all that, I could only hope the experience meant something special to Lauren. I waded through the crowd into the school and found Lauren so that we could head home for a little celebration. As we headed down the hallway, I was surprised at how often we were stopped by exuberant students wanting to say goodbye. They knew Lauren's name. They knew who she was. It felt monumental to me. Everything I had sought to accomplish for Lauren had been realized.

The added bonus was that even though I know these students will go off to their colleges, jobs, and new lives leaving Lauren behind, they will remember her. And, just maybe, when they encounter someone like Lauren again, they will be more inclined to accept them as part of the fabric of their lives, more inclusive than some of the adults we have encountered thus far.

PLATITUDES

2004—Lauren is 18 years old

When I learned about my daughter's developmental issues a few months after she was born, I didn't know what it would mean for her or for me. I just knew that our lives would be forever impacted by the fact that she was not going to have the intellectual or physical abilities of the average person. I could only see it as a tragedy, a horrible turn in our lives down a path that would only hold sadness and grief. What I didn't know during those first few wandering-in-shock years was just how severe Lauren's challenges would be. If I had, I think I would have been too paralyzed by the enormity of it all to begin to move forward.

The realization of the extent of Lauren's disability came slowly over years, piece by piece, within moments of undeniable truth. By the time the whole truth was apparent, I had forged a strong and protective bond with Lauren borne of more than just giving birth, but of weathering a hail of assaults on the possibilities for her future. I can now see that it was a kindness of sorts that the doctor originally predicted Lauren would not get past the functioning level of a seven-year-old. A seven-year-old walks, talks, feeds themselves, and has at least some self-care skills. I had thought that pronouncement was the end of the world. New-mother me could not have handled the revelation of what Lauren's actual challenges would turn out to be.

Over those revelatory years, I had learned not only the extent of Lauren's lifelong disabilities, but I also had come to understand that her life was not a tragedy. It was the challenges added to her life—intolerance, exclusion, lack of perceived value, lack of adequate supports—that created the heartbreak in her life.

I cannot change the intellectual and physical limitations that Lauren must live with, but I can try to change the world's understanding and reaction to those limitations. That insight has altered my concept of the path that my life will take in raising my daughter.

As a child, I had been known as the "No, thank you" kid. Painfully shy, saying no usually meant that people moved on to deal with the yeses and left me alone. I remained introverted as an adult, dreading gatherings where I didn't know people, content to stay in the background. I realized early in Lauren's journey that if I was going to be the mother that she needed, I couldn't be quiet and I couldn't be shy...about anything.

That means more than just speaking up and engaging with people who have an impact on Lauren's life; it also means taking Lauren to public places, even if it is just the grocery store or the mall. It took me a long time to get comfortable with that, but I need to include her in as much of life as possible. This requires learning to turn a blind eye to people's reactions as Lauren grows older and her mannerisms and vocalizations stray increasingly far from the norm.

Not everyone tries to avoid us. Fellow shoppers will often stop us in the grocery store to impart wisdom, such as, "God doesn't give us more than we can handle" and "You must be so strong." We've had more than our fair share of "God bless yous" imparted with understanding nods from people I'm pretty sure cannot possibly understand our lives. "You're a saint," has just as much capacity to annoy me as "I'm so sorry" said quietly over Lauren's head while they stare into my eyes. I know people think they are being kind, but I get so angry that they are offering condolences about the existence of my child.

For some people, a passing comment isn't enough. They stop us and relate their kinship with us because their second cousin once removed has a child with Down Syndrome, or their granddaughter in Iowa is deaf. They think this creates some kind of bond between us. It does not. It's like telling someone visiting from Italy, "Oh, you should meet my friend Maria. She's Italian too." We may share a label, an identity—caring about someone with a disability—but people with disabilities are incredibly diverse. They have a wide range of challenges and life experiences. Simply loving someone with a disability does not mean that the lives we are leading are remotely the same.

The most inappropriate comment we get (and it's happened many, many times) occurs when Lauren has a seizure. Someone, who I think is trying to be helpful will come over to us and say, "Are you OK?" And, then they'll continue, "My dog has seizures, too." I can rarely do more than stare at them. Do they not realize that they have just compared my daughter to their dog?

People do say some nice things, too. "What beautiful hair your daughter has!" or "It's nasty out today, do you need help?" I appreciate that they see us as people, not anomalies or objects of pity. I understand that it's hard for many people to not see Lauren as the result of a tragedy, an error in the unfolding of a human life. I can't say that, without the experience of raising Lauren, I would not be counted among them. But a view of Lauren from a distance is very different than up close and personal. Sure, Lauren's life is difficult. Yes, it has not been easy raising her. But, Lauren is not a tragedy; she is exceptional not because of her challenges but rather because she is a young woman who is smiley and stubborn, sweet and spirited. You can't tell that until you get to know her. So it's my job to dispel any idea that Lauren's life is tragic. If I cannot achieve that, I fear that, as an adult, Lauren will be relegated to the periphery of society.

Lauren's challenges can be handled, compensated for, and accepted. But that requires understanding, tolerance, and adequate supports be present in the community in which she lives. Lauren does not bemoan her disabilities. It is not the lack of common abilities that causes sadness and segregation in her life. It is the often inappropriate reaction of community members and the inadequate response of society that drains the color and quality from a life already dimmed by fate.

So, regardless of the stares, the odd comments, and annoyed glances when Lauren's vocalizations seem like just unnecessary noise, we shop, we go to church, we go to the Fourth of July parade. It has taken me time to adjust to the challenges that are part of who Lauren is. We need to give everyone else a chance to catch up.

WHAT THEN?

2005—Lauren is 20 years old

The age of 21, for most of us, is a peculiar mixture of both exciting possibilities and frightening uncertainties. The world is opening before us and we hope that only our imagination and our effort stands between us and the promise our futures can hold. My daughter, Lauren, will soon be turning 21, and we already know that her future holds very limited possibilities and particularly frightening uncertainties. There will be no college degrees or job. There will be no wedding or family of her own to look forward to. For Lauren, turning 21 means that an insecure future of dependency awaits her. Soon, she will age out of the entitlements of the education system. That little yellow school bus will no longer pick her up five mornings a week. And, what then? What will Lauren's life look like as an adult?

Her school expects Lauren to transition to a day program for adults with developmental disabilities. Because Lauren is non-verbal and non-ambulatory, group programs—especially ones with more than three or four people—have never worked out well for her. In school, she spends her days in a small group of students with needs similar to hers. When we've tried day camp or activity groups, Lauren was overshadowed and overwhelmed by others more active and more able to compete for attention. Lauren ended up relegated to the sidelines, bored and forgotten. I could not see Lauren spending the rest of her life—perhaps 40 or 50 years or more—in that kind of program. The school encouraged me to "just take a look" at the local day program that was prepared to meet Lauren's level of care.

I walked into a large, dimly lit room with gray walls and light gray floors. It smelled of some kind of cleaning solution shouting chemical more than clean. The high-ceilinged room was spacious, with utilitarian tables and chairs filling the corner to my right. The rest of the space was mostly empty except for the group of 15 or so men and women gathered around a television in a nook on my left. The sound on the television was set so low that I could only detect a murmur and occasional notes of music. Most of the people were sleeping, heads bent like drooping flowers as they sat in wheelchairs and on hard plastic chairs.

No one had greeted me when I came in the front door. Where were the staff? I suddenly heard people talking, their voices spilling through an open door in the far back corner. I headed there. Stepping into the space, I found three staff members chatting near desks covered in papers and binders. They were surprised to see me, even though I had made an appointment to visit that day. One, who introduced herself as the manager, showed me around (not that there was much I hadn't already seen). She listed the daily activities and field trips the participants took. While we were talking, a young woman wandered haphazardly around the room yelling unintelligibly, seemingly trying to communicate something to the indifferent staff. I thanked the manager for meeting with me and hurried outside to my car. I made it as far as the main road before I began sobbing.

There seemed to be no engagement, no purpose to the existence of that small group of disabled adults watching a movie even I could not hear. I could have caught the day program at a bad time, but should there be a bad time? The people huddled in front of that television seemed like the detritus left in an abandoned warehouse, forgotten inventory that hadn't been missed. Many of those people had been quite young, years spreading out before them swathed in impenetrable shrouds of boredom. I cannot relegate my daughter to spending each day watching the minutes of her life tumble into an interminable void.

Lauren's options are incredibly limited. It will be this program or staying home. Once you turn 21, government funding is no longer required to provide anything more than health insurance (Medicaid). Over the years, I have complained about the school system, special education, unwelcoming and unprepared educators, but at least I had something to complain about. The adult service system is significantly less adequate and more complicated. This will be a new system for me to learn and an even more critical one. Unless an individual with developmental disabilities has the ability to work, they are going to require a wide range of lifelong supports including residential, direct care, and transportation. Those supports are often beyond most family's physical and financial capabilities to provide for a lifetime. Waiting lists for any type of support are common. Waiting lists for residential services number in the thousands.

I fear that, for Lauren, adulthood will be devoid of safety, security, and permanence. I am glad that Lauren does not understand the uncertainty and risks of her future. I am absolutely terrified. When Lauren leaves school—her comfortable second home—long-established routines will disappear. As if someone has suddenly changed the channel, the plot of our lives will be dramatically different. What will she do with her days? Who will be in her life besides her family? How do we plan for the day when I can no longer care for her?

After 21 years of meeting 24/7 care needs, I have a clearer picture of what the infinite necessity of that care really means. It is overwhelming to contemplate, intensified by my lack of optimism that the supports and services that Lauren needs will be available in the years ahead. But they have to be, they just have to be, because her survival depends on it.

LIMITATIONS

2006—Lauren is 21 years old

The first day of kindergarten is still a vivid memory for me some 49 years later. I was terrified. Every day of those first five years of life, I had either been with a parent or a grandparent. Now, I was expected to get on this big, rumbling yellow bus all by myself and go to a place I didn't know to spend an entire morning with strangers. The horror! The bus driver assured my mother that if she could get me up the three steps into the bus, I could sit right next to her substitute motherly frame for the interminable, mile-long drive to school.

Apparently it took quite a while for me to adjust to being thrust out into the big wide world of school. My school picture that year shows a very sad little girl in a blue plaid dress, a white Peter Pan collar framing a pale face with woeful, red-rimmed eyes.

I had been sheltered by my parents, cocooned within a world of their protection. Starting school was the first big step in my life, and I just wasn't prepared for it. It had been scary and traumatic. Now, as parent to my own daughter, I'm trying to figure out how I can adequately prepare her for a big step in her life—leaving school. I don't want this huge change in her life to be distressing. It should be a time of discovery and growth for her, but I fear that losing the educational and social opportunities that school represents for her will mean that Lauren's world will shrink rather than expand with possibilities, narrow rather than broaden with opportunities.

Lauren's severe disabilities challenge her intellectually and physically. Her adult life will not include the things that most of us take for granted. But it should still be able to offer her a decent quality of life and stimulating activities. However, there are few options for her within our rural community. There's simply not much for her to do.

We've ruled out a day program for adults with developmental disabilities. I've tried, but I just don't see her spending five days a week in what would basically be, for Lauren's level of disability, day care. Volunteering? Maybe, but since Lauren does not use her hands purposefully, is non-verbal, and could not understand the altruism of the activity, she would be there in body but not personally contributing.

Lauren's adulthood will not be a traditionally productive one. That doesn't mean it can't be rich in other things. I just haven't yet figured out what those things will be. She needs relationships beyond family and the people paid to be in her life. She needs places to be, things to do, connections to her community. It will be the voices of other people and changes of scenery that will provide the color and stimulation in her life. It doesn't seem like a lot to build a life on, though. But maybe I'm gauging it too much on what I would want or need, not what Lauren wants.

And there's another issue limiting options—the noise. Lauren vocalizes to express herself. Those of us who know Lauren well understand what she's trying to communicate, but we cannot control where, when, or how loudly she makes her point. No amount of shushing, cajoling, or pleas for patience make any impression on Lauren. For someone who does not know Lauren, her vocalizations are just noise—irritating, inappropriate, and disruptive. I require a certain amount of tolerance by my fellow humans, but it's not always fair for Lauren to be affecting everyone else's experience of an activity or event. In the grocery store, at a public park or in a doctor's office, I think to myself, "Well, suck it up people, we're doing the best that we can here." But at a movie theatre, a church service, or a restaurant—I get it. A certain amount of behavior conformity is required and respectful. So, I'm careful about where Lauren goes, what the socially appropriate behavior is for that activity, and where the nearest exit is.

At Christmastime a few years ago, the American Boychoir was performing nearby. Since Lauren loves music, my husband and I thought attending a concert might be a nice treat for her for the holiday season. The accessible seating in the rear of the small theater was right next to the exit. Perfect. Unfortunately, we didn't know the choir was going to begin their performance while entering from the back of the theater through the door right next to us.

The first small boy led the line of others to a stop right beside Lauren, ready for his cue to proceed to the stage. On cue, he emitted a clear-as-a-bell, dulcet tone to start the first song, standing next to Lauren. She was thrilled and voiced her pleasure with a loud squeal...and continued voicing her pleasure. The acoustics in that theater were phenomenal—unfortunately. Since all of these young boys were now blocking the exit, all I could do was hold my hand over Lauren's mouth to try and stifle the sound to some degree until the last boy had proceeded up to the stage. As soon as the path cleared, my husband retreated into the lobby with Lauren where they listened to the rest of the performance.

We've spent a lot of time in lobbies over the years. Will Lauren basically spend her adulthood in the lobby of life? I worry that Lauren's life will be colorless and relegated to the fringes of others' existence if I cannot come up with something for her to do, someplace for her spend her days outside of home.

While I'm wracking my brain for an idea, I have to continually remind myself that I cannot use the same parameters to evaluate Lauren's adult experience as I do my own. My husband said that Lauren was very happy listening to the concert in the lobby. I need to listen to Lauren. I need to stop trying to prepare Lauren for the life that I think she should have and help her live the life that she wants. Since that is not something that she can verbalize, it will take time to figure out what that is. However, isn't that what every parent should do when their child becomes an adult? Listen and patiently guide and support that child in living the life they choose, not the one you've chosen for them? It's just so very hard when that child is unusually vulnerable, inadequately equipped, and will eventually need to live their life in a world so ill-suited to support them.

FOR YOUR CONVENIENCE

2007—Lauren is 22 years old

t was a fabulous idea—or so I hoped. I had racked my brain for ideas about what my daughter could do with her days now that special education classes would no longer be her go-to destination Monday through Friday. Since we had ruled out a day program, I needed to get creative.

I considered what Lauren likes to do—listen to music, be outdoors, and go to the mall. Shopping! Maybe I could build something around shopping! Maybe she could provide a service, like shopping for seniors who can't easily shop for themselves, which would allow her to give back in a small way. Lauren would have enough funding in her state budget, since she wasn't going to be attending a day program, with which I could hire someone to work with her Monday through Friday. I just needed to find some people for whom she could shop.

I called our county Office on Aging. I contacted other groups that served seniors. I provided flyers and details and waited for phone calls from sweet little old ladies who would just be thrilled to have someone shop for them. Crickets. Not one phone call. Now what?

Plan B refocused our efforts on busy, working moms—the moms who use their lunch hour to run to the store for the few items they need to get through the next few days. I contacted two businesses and told them of our plan. They said, "Sure, we'll give it a try." And, "For Your Convenience" was born.

I was quite proud of myself for finding something positive and productive for Lauren to do as an adult. It was rather entrepreneurial even though she wasn't getting paid to do anything. She was making a contribution to the well-being of her community by supporting some hard-working moms. This was a great first step in building an adult life for Lauren.

After interviewing a number of potential candidates, I hired a woman to work as Lauren's aide. I dropped shopping list forms and instructions off at the two businesses, and told them what days to expect Lauren and her aide, Nancy, to pick up their lists.

Lauren and Nancy would visit each business one day a week, pick up the women's shopping lists, go to the grocery store, do the shopping, and deliver the items to the women a few hours later. It all sounded great in theory, and it worked well for a while. The same women tended to use the service each week, and Lauren was able to interact with people she would ordinarily never have met. But grocery shopping with Lauren isn't easy. You need to push her wheelchair while pulling the grocery cart through the obstacle course of the store aisles. Then, you have to load the groceries and Lauren into her ramped van. When they delivered the groceries, Nancy would need to get the groceries and Lauren into the building so that Lauren would be able to interact with her "clients."

After about six months, the staff changed at one of the businesses and they dropped out. And Lauren was growing increasingly unhappy with the twice-weekly grocery store visits. She was really just along for the ride, since Nancy did all of the actual shopping. And Nancy was developing physical issues from the strain on her wrists and shoulders. After about a year, the downside far outweighed the upside. The bottom line: —Lauren was unhappy with the activity, so why continue?

Fortunately, by now Nancy knew Lauren well enough that she could come up with simple activities and excursions that Lauren seemed to enjoy far more than grocery shopping. They went to the park and the mall. They played games with Nancy's grandchildren. And at Nancy's house, they discovered that Lauren loves a colorful fish tank.

During this first year out of the busy, noisy, rambunctious days spent in a classroom with five other students, a teacher, four aides, and occasional therapists, we also learned something new about Lauren. I had been afraid that the quiet days of simply hanging out with one other person would not be stimulating enough for Lauren. But apparently the classroom had been too stimulating. As she became used to the new, quieter normal of her days, Lauren's head came up and she started making eye contact like never before. Unable to process the many voices and sounds and commotion of her school environment, Lauren had withdrawn. We had not realized this was happening. We thought Lauren was just being Lauren. Now, she seemed more engaged, more connected to the moments of her life. She blossomed right before our eyes.

If you don't know Lauren well, you might not notice the somewhat subtle changes. When I say "blossomed," I mean tiny blue forget-me-nots rather than a lush, crimson rose. You might not realize how significant it is to have Lauren make eye contact with me, no matter how fleeting. You might not understand why I stop dead in my tracks to watch Lauren turn her head to follow someone walking past her. This is significant. It is like a door firmly closed for so long has been opened just enough to peek inside, just enough to know that there is something worth seeking out behind that door.

There haven't been a lot of positives winding their way through the last 22 years of Lauren's life. I am so happy that we have learned that eliminating the clamor of too many people incessantly in her day has allowed Lauren to open up to the world just a bit more. This revelation has also confirmed that although "For Your Convenience" didn't work out, I've made the right decision in not selecting a day program for Lauren. She needs the quiet, flexible days she has found with Nancy in order to relax into the best Lauren that she can be.

WILL YOU BE MY FRIEND?

2008—Lauren is 23 years old

aving friends, people who choose to be in your life, adds a great deal to the quality of our lives. But friendship only truly works if it's a two-way thing. If it's not, the friendship usually lacks substance and longevity.

Friendship is something important that is missing from my daughter's life. Because of Lauren's severe disabilities, she can't actively contribute a great deal to maintaining friendship. She does contribute, but it's subtle and takes effort to understand, more effort than people seem to want to expend. People sometimes express an interest in how Lauren is doing and even offer to stop by for a visit. But that visit rarely materializes. I tried to start a friendship circle for her once—a group of people who care about the well-being of the person who is the focus of the circle and commit to regular interaction and contact. But half the people who committed to coming didn't show and the rest became too busy to attend regular meetings or engage with Lauren on their own.

Relationships wither if I do not become the permanent conduit between Lauren and someone else, which negates the greater purpose of Lauren having her own friends. The only proof the relationship ever existed becomes a face in a photograph in the rarely opened pages of one of Lauren's old photo albums.

It is worrying to me that most of the people in Lauren's life, except for family, are paid to be there. She needs those people, and they are incredible individuals who choose to do demanding and necessary work. But the relationship is a fragile one, its depth and length related to employment and what is going on in their own lives. They will come and go based on personal or professional needs, and Lauren's preferences will not be considered in the decision making.

During Lauren's high school years, two different aides were assigned to her. They not only facilitated Lauren's participation in activities, but learned to interpret her wordless communication and provide the most personal of care. These were both professional and undeniably intimate relationships.

The first aide, Sharon, arrived at our home with the little yellow school bus each morning, spent all day with Lauren, and returned with her in the afternoon. I was confident each morning that I was handing Lauren over to someone who truly cared about her. Sharon kept me well informed about the nuances of Lauren's days. She invited Lauren to her wedding. She gave her special gifts on holidays. Working on her degree at night for several years, Sharon eventually graduated and soon found the job she had been working toward. We were sad to see her go and anxious about who would take her place. But we wished her well, knowing she wasn't leaving the area, just changing jobs. At the time, we thought Sharon could continue to have a relationship with Lauren, who would find this transition difficult and unsettling.

Each day of Lauren's life was a seamless transition from my care to Sharon's. Now Lauren would have someone else feeding her and handling her body. Someone else would need to learn how she communicated and become familiar with her needs and preferences. Most of us have a hard time with change; for Lauren, it would be exponentially more difficult because she could not give instructions, answer questions, or even effectively complain. It never dawned on me that Sharon would not also be concerned about Lauren's transition to a new aide or that she would not want to make sure it was going well. However, we never saw her again. She never called to check on Lauren or communicated in any way. She seemingly wiped Lauren out of her life as easily and finally as an eraser wipes chalk off a blackboard.

Sandy took over as Lauren's aide. She was appalled at how Sharon had simply disappeared from Lauren's life. "What kind of a person does that?" she had exclaimed. Sandy was with Lauren for several years and played a valuable role in preparing Lauren to leave high school. After the last day of school, rife with teary remembrances and plans for summer lunches, Sandy also disappeared, and we never heard from her again.

How do I explain to Lauren the seeming ease with which these people left her behind? How do I explain to her that, to these people, it was just a job? They handled her body, put food in her mouth, spent most of the days of many years with her. To her, it was a relationship; to them, it was a paycheck.

I could make up excuses or possible reasons why Lauren's aides haven't kept in touch, but it's hard when I don't understand, either. The truly sad thing is this will probably be the norm in Lauren's life. Lauren will have a lifetime of dependency on people who will become keystones in her life, but she will not be as important in theirs. They will be able to leave her behind, and she will have no power to do anything about it or even ask why.

I fear that, one day, Lauren will be alone in the world with no one to love her, no one to care that she is safe, healthy, and happy. We have a small, unprolific family. Lauren is my only child, an only niece, an only cousin. Her care will be a lot to put on someone else's shoulders—a lot of responsibility and a lot of work. Who would volunteer to take this on? I get that. I really do.

Lauren will be dependent on people paid to be in her life to make decisions and direct her care. She will be unable to speak for herself, unable to advocate for her needs. Do any of us not fear being alone and dependent? We fear that old age could require us to rely on a caregiver who may or may not be interested in or concerned with our quality of life. For Lauren, this scenario is all but a given, long before she reaches old age.

I can leave instructions, detail my wishes for Lauren's care, but without my presence, they may only be dusty pieces of paper in some long-forgotten file. My concern is not just who will care for Lauren when I'm gone, it's who will care *about* Lauren when I'm gone. Lauren will require someone to care about her someday when I can no longer be there for her. That is why it is so important for Lauren to have friends who choose to be a part of her life.

Where is Mr. Rogers when you need him? In one of his straightforward little songs, he sang, "You are my friend, you are special to me." These nine simple words could make a huge difference in Lauren's life. Words that I hope Lauren will one day hear, because I fear that Mr. Rogers was right in saying, "Love is at the root of everything, love or the lack of it."

CARING FOR LAUREN

2010—Lauren is 24 years old

At 54, I find myself providing more diverse and more physically taxing care for my 24-year-old daughter than I did when she was a baby. Each day, her 5 foot, 3 inch, 100 pound body needs to be transferred from bed, to wheelchair, to stander, to toilet, to shower chair, to recliner, and back again throughout the day. Besides meeting physical care needs, I prepare her soft or pureed diet and feed her. I do her laundry and buy her clothing. I manage her seizure medications, medical needs, doctor's appointments, and insurance issues. I deal with case managers and paperwork. I manage caregivers—training, supervising, scheduling, and more paperwork. I arrange social activities, as well as figuring out what kind of music my nonverbal daughter likes and what television shows she enjoys. I am her nonstop advocate. I dance with her wheelchair to her favorite song. I paint her toenails. I kiss her goodnight. And in the dim light of too many early mornings, I hold her shaking body after yet another seizure.

But the years are creeping up on me, and I am tired. Chronic back and shoulder issues, migraines, and unrelenting fatigue are a constant presence. I've slept with a monitor next to my bed every night since Lauren was born. I sleep lightly, listening for each sound that could signal a seizure or other type of distress. *Is she breathing alright? Did she kick her covers off? Is she stuck in an uncomfortable position?* I'm up two or three or more times a night, checking on her.

And then there are the sleepless nights that I spend worrying. There has always been a lot to worry about. These days, I find that I worry less about how Lauren's challenges affect her and more about the limitations of the world around her and the instability of the systems required to protect her when I no longer can.

Not too long ago, I pulled the newspaper out of its bright yellow bag to find a front page story about a young woman named Kayla. She had no family who could care for her. Kayla had multiple severe disabilities much like Lauren. She lived with strangers and died from lack of care.

A 28, Kayla weighed just 48 pounds. A caseworker reported finding her dirty, with her shoes on the wrong feet. Her room was filthy and smelly. She was starved, abused, and forgotten by the people that should have been overseeing her welfare.

In Lauren's life, she eats healthy, well-balanced meals. She has stylish clothes and pretty clips to hold her dark curls off of her face. She smiles each morning when I spritz her favorite perfume on the back of her neck. She sleeps in a canopied bed with a fluffy, flower-strewn comforter. This is a decent quality of life. It is not fancy or extravagant. It is comfortable, clean, and caring. How can I guarantee Lauren has at least that for the rest of her life? What happened to Kayla could just as easily happen to Lauren.

It takes a special kind of person to take on the care of someone like Lauren or Kayla. Apparently, the right people were not taking care of

Kayla. We have been fortunate so far; we have had wonderful people caring for Lauren.

Over the last seven years, we have hired at least 25 people to work for Lauren in the role of caregiver, which means we've interviewed at least 150 people. Some lasted one day, some have been with us for years. Lauren and I always interview potential candidates together. She can't verbally express her opinion, but I can tell by her reactions to the interview exactly what she's thinking. Although her level of care is similar to a small child's, she demands the respect of a young woman, with opinions, interests, and an adult life to lead.

If the interviewee is talking to her like a baby or fawning all over her, she'll give me her version of an eye roll. If they're loud and never stop talking, she shuts down and acts like they're not there. If they're cowering in their chair and I can't get them to talk, she'll fill in the blanks with her own vocalizing. If she likes someone, she'll smile and steal glances at them from under her long, black lashes.

When Lauren turned 18, she started receiving funding with which we could hire caregivers to work consistent shifts during the week. I would place an ad in our local newspaper for two or three days and usually receive 30 or 40 replies from which I'd choose a dozen or so candidates to interview. That worked well for a few years until the responses to ads started to dwindle. In the last year or two, an ad in the paper receives perhaps one or two responses. I've tried flyers, online ads, Facebook, word of mouth.... with few results. If you need to hire a caregiver to work with someone who has a developmental disability but can walk and talk and feed themselves, it isn't as difficult. But for someone with significant care needs like Lauren, the well is running dry.

Caring for someone like Lauren involves a lot of responsibility. It's physically taxing and requires a lot of patience. The pay rates, set within certain funding parameters, are usually far below what they should be. People who choose this work often work two or three jobs in order to survive and provide for their families. Often there are no benefits and no advancement possibilities.

Someday soon, Lauren will need to rely on caregivers for all of her care. This issue of being able to find and maintain qualified, caring staffing is a major concern. A crisis in finding caregivers was forecasted years ago. It's a result of many factors but primarily those inadequate pay rates. Without a significant investment in this workforce, the problem will continue and intensify as Lauren gets older.

I think she should always have a choice of who she spends her days with and who she allows to provide the most intimate of care. But that may not be possible. Many providers are hiring people they wouldn't have considered a few years ago, just because they must have bodies in caregiving positions. Quality of care and quality of life cannot help but suffer. I would provide all of Lauren's care myself before I would let that happen, but that is not realistic. I can't do that now, how will I do it when I'm even older?

The first step in addressing this crisis in caregiving is to raise pay rates to a level commensurate with the responsibilities and duties required of the position. There are people who would like to do this work, but can't afford to because they have mouths to feed. Raising pay rates sufficiently may never happen in a system already strapped for funding. Also, these caregivers are primarily women (a historically undervalued group), providing care (a historically undervalued job), for people with developmental disabilities (a historically undervalued segment of the population). Very few besides the families that love them are going to think their care should be a priority. In fact, the Bureau of Labor Statistics—a federal agency that provides essential statistical data to the American public, the U.S. Congress, other federal agencies, and state and local governments—does not even have a classification for the caregivers that work with individuals with developmental disabilities.

This is a vastly different job than a home health aide or personal care attendant, but that fact is not recognized.

The people who support individuals with developmental disabilities must be caregivers and advocates for individuals with a wide range of intellectual, physical, medical, and behavioral challenges. They teach daily living skills, social skills, and workplace skills. They must complete extensive training to work specifically with this population, complete complex documentation, and often work independently in community settings. Providing this kind of support requires skill, dedication, and a high level of responsibility.

Lauren asks for very little. She needs to be clean, fed, comfortable, and folded into the life of her community with dignity and respect. She can't achieve that on her own. She needs caregivers who can choose to help her do that without sacrificing their own well-being. I don't think that's asking for too much. I just want what every other parent wants for their child. I want Lauren to be happy and safe. I want Lauren to continue to live the life that she doesn't seem to find wanting.

One day, I won't be there to tell Lauren's caregivers how truly special she is, to tell them her story, relate the highs and lows of her life, help them to see the sweet, feisty young woman struggling to live her best life. All I can do is hope that I find some way to assure that other caring hands will wash the sleep from her eyes each morning and make sure that she has what she needs each day. But until I find a way to guarantee that, it will be one more worry to keep me awake in the dark of those long, sleepless nights.

A HOME OF HER OWN

2011—Lauren is 26 years old

t's taken almost a year of preparation, but my daughter has moved into her own home. I never thought that I would say those words. I wasn't sure that Lauren could survive without my daily guiding presence, and I couldn't picture her living somewhere without me. For that matter, I couldn't picture myself living somewhere without her.

The path to Lauren actually moving into her home was a complicated one. Lauren needs an accessible home and 24/7 care. We could have opted for a group home when an opening became available, but I did not think Lauren would be happy or receive the level of care she needs in a group home. And, truthfully, I wanted to choose where Lauren lives, with whom she lives, and who cares for her. I can't leave those things up to someone else's judgment. I've managed to get Lauren to the age of 26, happy, healthy, and safe—despite multiple severe disabilities. It has not been easy. I'm not going to risk her well-being by giving up control of those critical pieces of her adult life.

Without the "prepackaged" aspects of a provider-run group home, it means that I have to organize all of the pieces—direct-care staffing, housing, utilities, etc.—by myself. It's doable, but it's not easy. All of those pieces have different funding sources or assistance programs. Since Lauren's income is limited to her Supplemental Security Income (SSI) of about $700 a month, she will forever need help with her rent, utilities, food, and, most importantly, 168 hours of care a week.

Lauren has two developmental disability-specific funding sources that should cover the hours of care that she needs if we hire people ourselves instead of through an agency. It will require that I hire and train her staff, handle paperwork, manage scheduling, and cover empty shifts as needed.

Financial help with rent, utilities, and food is linked to government programs available to all citizens if they qualify, so Lauren is in competition for limited funding with other needy groups. Lauren will need this assistance for a lifetime with no ability to change her circumstances. She is never going to be able to work. She is never going to get "better." Her income will never significantly increase. And there is no indication that Lauren's lifespan will be shortened by her disability.

I knew that, in order to afford a home of her own, Lauren would need a "rental assistance voucher." The availability of vouchers is dependent on sporadic releases of funding in particular areas, and it was the critical piece of the housing puzzle I would need to complete. Timing is everything and, fortunately, just when I found a place for Lauren to live, vouchers were released in our county and Lauren was able to get one. If she hadn't, it could have been years before she would be able to get one.

The next hurdle was applying for utility assistance—electric, cooling, heating—and food stamps. But—and it's a big "but"—we wouldn't know how much Lauren would actually get from these resources until a few months after she moved into her home. Since the amounts are subject to change on a yearly basis, there was no way to prepare more than a budget based on guesses.

All I can do is take the leap and hope that the numbers will work out. If we as Lauren's parents provide any financial assistance, it is counted as income and affects the levels of aid she receives. That would mean she would need even more of our assistance, which would then be counted as income and...you can see it's a vicious circle. So if the numbers don't work out, Lauren will be moving back to our home, and I will be back to square one in figuring out Lauren's long-term care.

I have been feeling a growing sense of urgency that I needed to get Lauren settled into an adult life sooner than later. A very wise lady who also has a daughter with severe disabilities once told me, "Get Lauren settled somewhere before you have to. Don't leave it until you have no choice. That way, if the situation doesn't work, you have time to make changes." I am closing in on 60, my husband on 80. I am struggling with Lauren's physical care. It is time.

July fifth was a typical, warm summer day in New Jersey, and it was moving day for Lauren. The fact that it was one day after Independence Day wasn't lost on me. I had no idea how Lauren would react to this move. I had been spending time with her in her new home, getting her used to the new spaces, doing some painting, moving her things in gradually over the course of a few days. I had planned to slowly transition her into her new home. She'd spend a few days in her new home, then return to my home for a few days, lengthening her stay in her own home until she was comfortable. But, from the first day she moved in, Lauren was ecstatic. In fact she was so happy that I never followed through on my strung out schedule designed to acclimate her to what I thought could be a traumatic change. She is on her own and she loves it.

I have had a much harder transition than Lauren did. Her room divested of her treasures, assorted shoes lying about, and pictures of the people who have loved and cared for her, is simply a room. That room, which had been so full of Lauren's constant noise, too many seizures, and the breezy voice of Kenny Chesney, is now simply a room.....an incredibly quiet room. In fact, the entire house has a stillness as if she took the energy of our home with her when she left.

Lauren was my reason to get out of bed each morning. Her schedule created the guideposts of my day. I know she is not here, yet I listen for her. Especially at night, I wake at some perceived sound, prepared to run to her realizing that she is not here to make a sound.

Of course, I'm at Lauren's several times a week, checking on her, taking care of the details of her life, sneaking a hug when she lets me. And then I drive home through the winding roads that connect my home and her home, with tears running down my face. I feel guilty and my heart aches when I leave her. I have to remind myself that she is happy. Despite all of the challenges in this young woman's life, she is happy. I know I've done the right thing in organizing an adult life for her. She has wonderful caregivers, a comfortable home, everything that she needs. I made sure of that. But it's not me styling her hair each morning, fluffing those soft brown curls just so. It's not me fixing her turkey sandwich the way I've always done. It's not me turning off her light each night. If she needs me, she cannot call out for me. And I feel selfish that I am not with her every moment to ease her way through this challenged life that I have given her. Is it my responsibility to prepare her to live without me? Or, is it my responsibility to dedicate my every waking, and sleeping, moment to personally assuring her comfort and safety? Somehow, it's both and that's impossible. I know that. And still, I feel guilty.

So when I get home to my empty, quiet, Lauren-less house, I dry my tears. More often than not there is paperwork to be done, phone calls to make, emails to send to keep her life on track. It's obvious that she still needs me, but now it's somewhat at arm's length. And the next day when I call to check on her, I can hear her laughing in the background. Lauren is home and she is most definitely happy.

MR. TURTLE

2012—Lauren is 27 years old

When my daughter was 18 months old, her occupational therapist suggested that I pick up a pull toy that we could use to work on skills at home. The next day, while out running errands with Lauren and my sister-in-law, I asked her to sit in the car with Lauren while I ran into a store to get the toy. I remember sliding back into the driver's seat and handing my sister-in-law the bag saying, "All I could find was this stupid turtle." Little did I know what a big role that little turtle would play in Lauren's life.

Mr. Turtle was made of hard Fisher-Price plastic. He had a green body, sunny yellow shell, and light blue feet. A white sailor hat was perched above painted-on eyes. A wiry yellow plastic string attached below his chin provided something to pull. Lauren loved the feel of the string in her fingers. She wouldn't necessarily use it to pull the toy purposefully, but she would at least hold it, a major accomplishment.

Out of all of the toys I bought her over the years, Mr. Turtle was by far her favorite. Some kids have a security blanket; Lauren had a security turtle. He went everywhere with us: doctor's visits, vacations, church. The only place he didn't go was to school.

As Lauren grew, Mr. Turtle began to take on other roles. We had tried various methods to help non-verbal Lauren to communicate. We decided to try taking photos of her red cup, various toys, and even the toilet, and then ask her to choose between two pictures. The only time she would respond was if we showed her a picture of Mr. Turtle and something else. Then she would place her hand on the picture of Mr. Turtle. After a while, Lauren began using Mr. Turtle to communicate, dropping him on the floor to get someone's attention. You'd have to guess what she wanted, but if you didn't figure it out, she'd just drop him again.

Mr. Turtle became a pseudo ambassador for Lauren. Since they always traveled as a pair, he became something that people who wanted to interact with Lauren but didn't know what to say could talk about. Small children found her more approachable because the turtle was so non-threatening and looked like something they might want to play with, too.

He also created a "theme" in Lauren's life. It was hard for people who wanted to buy Lauren a gift to know what to buy. But if you knew about Mr. Turtle, it gave you ideas. People started to buy her turtles—big ones, small ones, stuffed ones, musical ones, ones made of shells and silver and clay and glass and jade and wood, pictures of turtles, turtle flags, turtle wind chimes, turtle Christmas ornaments, turtle planters, and turtle refrigerator magnets. I could go on, but you get the idea. The turtle had provided a link for friends and family to use to connect with Lauren.

The Mr. Turtle that Lauren spends her days with now is not the same Mr. Turtle that I originally bought. Yes, Mr. Turtle and his descendants have had some adventures. The original guy lost a leg from one too many drops to the floor. His son cracked right down the middle from overuse and old age. One of the grandsons was decapitated by the van ramp when he suddenly rolled away while it was opening. That little sailor hat popped off like a cork out of a bottle of champagne.

In Lauren's late teens, Fisher-Price stopped making Mr. Turtles. I didn't want to contemplate a world without Lauren's faithful companion. I asked everyone I knew to look in their basements and attics for long-forgotten toys of their children. Soon, people started calling to let me know that they had found a Mr. Turtle at a garage sale or thrift store, and Lauren's collection grew. She currently has 11.

There are some people that think it's wrong for Lauren to still be interacting with a toy designed for small children or that it's not age appropriate. But I think that's short-sighted and judgmental. They may think it's just a toy, but that is their negative interpretation of a piece of plastic. It is much more to Lauren. Mr. Turtle gives voice to her thoughts and is constant in his presence, unlike some of the people in her life. He reaches out to pull others toward her in ways she cannot, giving new meaning to his original function as a pull toy.

In the end, it's not about what anyone else thinks, it's about what makes Lauren happy. If it's holding onto the string of a small green turtle that sports a jaunty sailor hat, I'll make sure there are heirs waiting in line to serve.

INDISPENSIBLE

2015—Lauren is 30 years old

E veryone wants to think that they're irreplaceable. Not me. In fact, it terrifies me. Despite my daughter's severe disabilities, she has been happily living life as an adult in her own home for six years. But Lauren's success and stability comes at a price—my constant oversight and involvement. I am as critical to her life as the oxygen she breathes and the water she drinks.

Each week I make the short drive from my home to Lauren's at least twice. I check her overall appearance and mood. I debrief the caregiver, rotating my visits to interact with all five staff as often as possible. I make sure that her home is clean, answer questions, and brainstorm any problems. I check on the care notes each shift leaves in Lauren's journal to make sure that she's eating, eliminating, and sleeping. I get a text or phone call each time Lauren has one of the two to five seizures she has each month, and I follow up later in the day to make sure she's recuperating.

I schedule all of Lauren's medical appointments. I accompany her to appointments with binders of my carefully kept notes and charts, but more importantly, my knowledge of the lifetime of details related to the care that each different doctor provides. Lauren requires equipment—a wheelchair, stander, and shower chair—that all have to be maintained, repaired, and replaced. Having to replace something, or even repair it for that matter, means phone calls, paperwork, waiting, and incessant follow ups. We needed to replace Lauren's wheelchair recently. The process took six months. It was a record, the fastest we've ever been able to obtain a new chair. But, there is a problem with the armrests and we've been waiting five months for a repair.

I also keep an eye on her van. Ten years ago, we replaced Lauren's last accessible van with an adapted Honda minivan. It was very expensive. The cost of the adaptation nine years ago, on top of the cost of the van, was more than $15,000. It's probably closer to $20,000 by now. So, I'm vigilant about maintenance and repairs. We need to keep this van in good condition for as long as possible.

Lauren depends on a system of government supports and services that has been going through a lot of changes. I need to attend meetings, read the latest updates on changes and new rules, and adapt Lauren's adult life as best I can to accommodate changes. When Lauren first moved into her home, we were able to work out a budget that just covered her expenses by combining her SSI, individual budgets from two different state disability departments, and rental, heating, cooling, and food assistance. The fallout from one of those system changes is that the state has now stopped paying for some things they paid for when we worked out Lauren's original budget. I had to figure out how, or if, there was a way to accommodate that change. It could easily have derailed her entire living situation, but with some juggling, so far, she's been able to manage.

The price you pay for choosing to "self-direct" your funding instead of opting for a provider-run program and/or group home is the ongoing management of multiple funding streams. It's a major challenge since they all have different rules, different timelines, and are overseen by different federal and state agencies.

In March, we were notified that it was time to renew Lauren's rental assistance. That meant submitting a packet of compiled paperwork to the Department of Community Affairs. In July, we were notified that they were processing Lauren's paperwork and the documents I provided in March were now too old. They needed more current ones.

In April, we received a notice that we needed to renew Lauren's application for the Supplemental Nutrition Assistance Program (SNAP). I compiled a packet of documents very similar to the rental assistance paperwork and sent that off to the county Board of Social Services. They will then call me at some point to review the paperwork on the phone. I have to explain Lauren's living situation—a severely developmentally disabled young woman living in her own home—each time because there's a different person handling her renewal each year.

Last fall, we received a notice that Lauren's Low Income Home Energy Assistance Program (LIHEAP) renewal would occur automatically because she had been renewed for SNAP. Two months later, I realized that there was no customary LIHEAP credit on her electric bill. When I called the agency handling LIHEAP, I was told that someone must have "forgotten" to put Lauren's application in and that she would need to apply all over again.

I filled out the application and, once again, gathered up supporting documentation and sent it off. By the time the application was processed, Lauren had gone three months without this critical assistance. She doesn't dare miss paying an electric bill. The electric company had originally refused to put the account in Lauren's name, which is a prerequisite to applying for assistance, because she had no credit history. I had to contact the New Jersey Board of Public Utilities to get them to intervene on her behalf. Now we have to be very careful not to give the electric company any excuse to pull her account.

Recently, there were major changes to the state-mandated process we need to follow in order to hire staff for Lauren. These changes caused unmanageable issues and necessitated contracting with a home health agency instead of self-hiring in order to cover the necessary shifts. But one of the state budgets (luckily the smaller one) doesn't allow for the use of an agency, so I still need to deal with the ongoing problems caused by the new process, just on a smaller scale. Staying on top of staffing is imperative, and I must keep staff and their shifts coordinated, process timesheets, and make sure that sick days, vacation days, and personal days are covered. Lauren can never be left alone.

Bringing an agency on board at this point in Lauren's life actually works for us because it was becoming almost impossible to find people to hire ourselves. Right now, Lauren has amazing women caring for her, but the staffing shortage keeps getting worse. If we cannot find adequate staffing, someone with Lauren's level of need could easily end up in a nursing home. There are already reports of this happening to other people.

Monthly, I meet with or have required phone contact with multiple case managers. However, they never speak to each other and are responsible for different things. I am the conduit that links them together. Otherwise, there could be gaps in meeting Lauren's needs, each one thinking the other has it covered. In addition, Lauren has had 11 different people in those roles in the last two years. If something was not right with her care or living situation, they wouldn't know her well enough to know there was a problem. How would they know that she is looking thinner or is trying to communicate something in her wordless vocalizations and gestures if they have had no time to get to know her?

There are times when I need to drop what I'm doing and run to Lauren's. It doesn't happen often, but it happens; a caregiver gets sick during her shift, something breaks on Lauren's wheelchair, Lauren seems to be coming down with something. I'm fortunate that I work part-time from home so that I can run when I have to, schedule meetings and appointments as required, keep up with paperwork, and cover a shift if we just cannot work out the scheduling. But if you take me out of the equation, who does all of these tasks? Who takes responsibility for Lauren's well-being and keeps the myriad facets and fragments of her life running smoothly?

My role in Lauren's life—and the roles of other parents like me— is a critical but finite piece of the support-system puzzle. The system designers, who encourage self direction for individuals and creativity among their families, neglected to include an alternative for when that resource no longer exists. I've sat in the meetings where they talked about "natural supports" (meaning mom, dad, siblings, and even neighbors) that would fill this role, as if it was a universal resource in everyone's life...for their lifetimes. Lauren is my only child; when I die or become disabled myself, she will be alone. She shouldn't have to lose a life in which she has been safe, healthy, and happy because I can no longer manage her life. She shouldn't risk institutionalization because I can no longer be her advocate.

Supporting Lauren's adult life is something that I do willingly because she is thriving in the life I have assembled for her. Sustaining this alternative to a group home is not an impossible job, but it is definitely an unnecessarily complex one that few families could take on or would have the resources to support. It bothers me that Lauren has this option only because I have had the ability to devote myself to Lauren's needs. Other individuals may not have the same option because of their family's limitations, not their own.

Who will take over my support role for Lauren when I am unable to continue? No child's survival should depend on the perpetual life of their parent. Someday, Lauren will not have lost her funding, services, supports, caregivers, or place to live. She will just have lost her mom. But for Lauren, that could mean losing her own life, as well.

INCOMPLETE

2018—Lauren is 33 years old

Ulysses spent many years at war, and 10 long years trying to return home from war. Throughout those years, he encountered detours and challenges, Cyclops and Circe, cannibals and all manner of delays. When he was old, tired of leading, tired of the battles, tired even of the seas upon which he spent so much of his life, he picked up an oar and started walking. He walked until he found people who didn't know who he was or even what an oar was. There he made his home and lived out his days in peace.

There are days—too many days—when I completely understand Ulysses' quest for a world far different from his own. There are days when I want to forget the turmoil and move past the lingering angst of difficult years. Like a blackboard washed free of not only the words scrawled on its surface but even the dusty remains of past phrases, I wish I could wash away the remnants of struggles and failures, leaving open a space for a future uninformed by the weighty history of things painful to remember.

For the last 33 years, my days have been informed by the titles "mom of a child with developmental disabilities," and "disability advocate." For every one of those years, my daughter's disability has been what has defined and focused my existence. It has required a shy, would-be artist become a warrior like Ulysses—a warrior for my child's survival.

I feel that this focus on disability has left incomplete spaces within me. All of my energies have been funneled into the skills and knowledge that I need to care for Lauren, to help her address the incomplete spaces of her own. There has been no time, no energy left to figure out what I wanted or what I needed. I don't mean that as a complaint. It's a simple statement of fact. I do not begrudge the time or effort that I devote to Lauren. She has brought out depths of love and commitment in me that I didn't know I possessed. But it doesn't mean that I don't have my "if only" moments.

I know that meeting the needs caused by Lauren's disability has resulted in increased abilities for me. I had no choice but to learn, grow as a person, and become bold. But every once in a while, I wonder what else I could have been if "disability" were not woven so completely into the fabric of who I am. I can't separate myself from it anymore. My friends are mostly other mothers of children with disabilities. I enter a building and judge its accessibility, even if Lauren is not with me. I have a permanent Google alert for news on disability subjects. I am a constant advocate, vigilant for threats to services and vocal about unmet support needs.

Perhaps without Lauren in my life, I would have traveled, became a designer, or learned to ski. Or perhaps I would have done none of those things because without being forced to speak up for a child that couldn't speak for herself, and without learning that I had a voice and ideas and power, I probably would have remained the timid wallflower I had always been.

And I have to admit, most of those "if only" moments that I indulge in are about the things that I have been unable to share with Lauren, not about what I could have achieved without her in my life. Things like ballet recitals, bike riding, college tours, and wedding planning all would have been potential fodder for beautiful, positive memories that will never happen. That is what feels particularly incomplete, as if that part of both of us is missing, that connection born of what would have been the normal experiences of a middle-class mother and daughter in suburban New Jersey.

Lauren may not know what could have been. But I certainly do. I accepted long ago that Lauren's life would be different than most and that she would never walk or speak. That is the reality of my waking moments. In sleep, I sometimes dream of a Lauren with her many challenges swept away.

I will wake with a feeling of lightness, which is unnatural for me. Confused by the absence of my usual morning dreads, I will search for the source of my glee and the dream will filter into my consciousness. I see Lauren walking toward me across the pristine, white carpeting of her bedroom, words spilling from her mouth like a waterfall. I don't remember what she says; it doesn't matter. It is her sparkling eyes that are the most startling window into a Lauren unclouded by the restraints of disability. I struggle to hang on to the wisps of a reality neither of us will ever experience, but like all dreams, it vanishes like smoke drifting though my fingers, and a feeling of loss ensues.

The dream always makes me feel a little guilty, as if in sleep, my subconscious is trying to fix the parts of Lauren it perceives as incomplete. But in the light of day, I know that Lauren's incomplete parts are simply like negative space—the space within, between, and around an object that an artist uses to balance and define his focal point. This space, in Lauren's case, is indeed not a void, but rather adds necessary and welcome definition to the borders of her existence. It complements the complex composition that is purely Lauren. But others may see that negative space as defining what is missing and who she cannot be. When Lauren was a baby, when this disability life sentence was revealing itself, it was all that I saw, as well. But what was eventually revealed to me was that Lauren, despite her challenges, would teach me far more than I would teach her.

Without words, Lauren has guided me to the understanding that who she is— is simply enough. She has neither wealth nor professional achievement, nor does she aspire to be anything greater than she is. Yet she smiles every day, enjoys the simple pleasures of her life—her music, her fish tank, a walk in the park—and when she closes her eyes each night, her face is peaceful and calm. Lauren somehow inherently knows what is important in life. She is not influenced by peer pressure, media, or avarice of any kind. She is unfailingly true to herself.

It is ironic that for someone with such significant cognitive challenges, Lauren epitomizes the much sought after "mindfulness." She lives in the moment, neither depressed by the events of the past nor anxious about the future. I recognize the value of that and wish that I could emulate her. But instead, my mind strays to ever-present worries constantly available for viewing like a film loop in my mind, worries about the funding needed to support Lauren's long-term care, about the quality of that care, and about what will happen to her when I'm gone. Worry about the things that are missing, not in Lauren, but in her world.

Although Lauren has taught me that all you really need to be happy is a decent place to live, your basic needs met, and people who care about your well-being, I know that those things are not a guarantee in her future. We citizens of this world have not yet made taking care of each other a priority. Maybe we never will.

I am growing weary of fighting ongoing battles to have the needs of the Laurens in this world recognized and respected. I have been participating for far too many years in vain efforts to get the supports available to people with disabilities and their families improved. Yes, at least we have something. We are not left to the impossible task of meeting diverse and intense needs completely on our own. But I think we can do so much better.

Ulysses was incredibly optimistic to believe that if he walked far enough, he could find what he was looking for. Unfortunately, I'm more pessimistic than he is. If one day I grab hold of the handles of Lauren's wheelchair and start walking, I don't think there is anywhere in this world—yet—that we could find what we need to start over again, a place where we both could look forward to peaceful years ahead and never need to feel that either we, or our world, was incomplete.

AFTERWORD

In my opinion...

have spent almost every day of my daughter's life attempting to meet and plan for her special needs. I have also been seriously involved in advocacy efforts to improve supports and promote better policies for individuals like Lauren for almost 30 years. Most families simply cannot provide care for individuals with significant needs without help, nor can they plan for the future without acceptable options for meeting long-term care needs. Three decades into my role as an advocate, I have unrelenting concerns about the direction of the disability service system, what it has not yet accomplished, and the critical issues it must address.

Providing supports and services for individuals with developmental disabilities is an expensive business. Many states have long waiting lists for services (whether they admit it or not), and many people are underserved. In an effort to bring more money into state coffers, 33 states, including my own New Jersey, have decided to avail themselves of the Medicaid expansion offered under the Affordable Care Act. For people with developmental disabilities, this means that, because of the ability to take advantage of federal Medicaid matching funds, more dollars will be available for services and supports. But there's a catch: states have to adhere to federal Medicaid rules about what those services can be, and monies cannot be used for housing, utilities, or food. The entire system becomes divided into a specific menu of services supported by Medicaid dollars and a piecemeal range of options for funding other costs critical to living an adult life.

What has been an effort to bring in more funding to improve the availability of services and to serve more people has been effectively strangled by the rules limiting the use of that funding. Those rules do not allow the funding to support a cohesive plan to meet the essential needs of a large portion of the developmentally disabled population. Instead, it is necessary to cobble together funding from multiple resources in order to adequately meet all the needs of an adult life. Medicaid monies, specifically from Home and Community Based Services (HCBS) waivers promote community living as the ideal. But those monies cannot truly support community-based lives unless they support all the necessary facets of a life in the community, including residential costs. However, Medicaid monies do support residential expenses if an individual lives in an institution or nursing home. The logic of that escapes me.

Even though Medicaid will not pay for housing-related expenses in the community, they have restrictions on where someone can live and still receive other Medicaid-funded supports. As parents and providers try to come up with creative options to meet long-term, adult housing needs—there aren't enough group homes or other options for the individuals who need them—their creativity is thwarted by Medicaid rules about how many people with disabilities can live together in a group home, in the same building, or in any type of housing arrangement. Medicaid "Settings Rules" (requirements about the qualities of the setting in which HCBS waivers can be provided) are contributing to the lack of desperately needed housing that can meet the diverse needs of adults with developmental disabilities.

However, it's not only Medicaid that imparts limitations on an individual's choices about their life. There are now 19 "Employment First" states that have official policies on employment for people with disabilities. That policy in New Jersey states, "Employment in the general workforce should be the first and preferred option for individuals with disabilities receiving assistance from publicly funded systems." It is required that all individuals eligible to receive funding from the NJ Division of Developmental Disabilities include in their service plan "at least one employment outcome, even if the individual is not pursuing employment at the time of the Individual Service Plan."

One example of a person navigating this system is Stacy, a woman in her early 40s who is severely disabled. Stacy rarely leaves her home, is tube fed, does not communicate in any significant way, and responds little to her environment. The support coordinator (case manager) informed her mother, "If we don't include something on employment, they won't approve Stacy's plan and she'll lose her funding. Without this funding, Stacy's 80-year-old mother knows that Stacy will end up in a nursing home. So, she agrees to the coordinator's suggestion that they put, "Will learn to wake up to an alarm clock" as a skill Stacy will work on to prepare for employment.

There is just so much wrong with this scenario. It absolutely reeks of a lack of respect for both Stacy and her devoted mother. Practically, Stacy does not know what a job is, what work is, or what money is. For that matter, she doesn't know what an alarm clock is or that the ringing means she's supposed to wake up and get ready for her day...which, of course, she can't do either.

In addition to scenarios like Stacy's, there are individuals, who had certain types of jobs, or who worked in special group programs where their inability to produce at a normal level or speed was accommodated, who have now lost those positions. Working at these jobs meant they could not meet the Employment First stipulation that they must earn "the greater of minimum or prevailing wages with commensurate benefits," and their employment must occur "in a typical work setting where the employee with a disability interacts or has the opportunity to interact continuously with co-workers without disabilities, has an opportunity for advancement and job mobility, and is preferably engaged full-time."

Some individuals working in settings not in line with those requirements may have brought home as little as $5 or $10 a week, but it was still money they had earned and a source of pride. For them, it wasn't about being held to a standard of productivity, it was about participating in something productive and having even a little something to show for it. Now, that is being denied them. The alternative for individuals who cannot perform at a level to gain regular employment is to attend a day program or sit at home. One young man attending a day program complained to me recently, "They took away my job. I just fall asleep doing this stuff," gesturing toward the painting projects and puzzles on the tables around him. But don't forget, he'll still be required to work on employment skills that he will most likely never be allowed to use in order to maintain his funding for any type of support.

Of course, people with developmental disabilities should not be exploited. Of course, they should absolutely receive whatever assistance they need to gain workplace skills and have the opportunity to be employed and fairly compensated. But the Employment First rules disrespect a large portion of the developmentally disabled population. Those rules require that individuals only be employed at a level that many are not capable of achieving—and effectively denigrate the level that they can achieve. People are required to prepare to work even if they cannot understand what "work" is. Proponents of Employment First insist that everyone can work. That is simply insulting to many individuals with developmental disabilities. And for others, it dangles the potential of work while restricting access. This policy reflects another example of logic not being part of this system.

These counterintuitive rules seem to be the new theme running throughout the design of a new generation of services and supports. In a laudable effort to bring in much-needed monies for supports and services, systems are being designed around the purported quest to protect the rights of individuals to be all that they can be, but they have forgotten about the rights of individuals to live with respect and dignity despite what they are not.

I am all for choice and control, the buzzwords that swarm these new programs and policies, but that is not what these policies are achieving. Instead, they are presenting narrow parameters within which what you need hopefully resides. If you need something that does not fall into specific guidelines, you are out of luck in systems that depend on federal dollars without additional state dollars available to fill in the gaps. The terms "choice" and "control" then become merely a veil obscuring the obvious inadequacies and roadblocks limiting the necessary range of options required by all levels of this diverse population.

There are also concerns about the recognition of that diversity. Policymakers seem to be in denial that there is a large segment of the developmentally disabled population that has intensive, lifelong care needs. Those with severe intellectual, physical, or behavioral disabilities are going to need high levels of long-term support. But policymakers seem focused on achievement and independence, avoiding recognition of the undeniable need of some for adequate care and ongoing protection. For example, new systems are causing individuals who have been living in the community to end up in nursing homes, not because their needs cannot be, and have not been, met in the community, but because community-based funding changes no longer support their lives there. Individuals with significant behavioral needs are being placed with providers unable or insufficiently compensated to meet their needs.

The result is abuse, neglect, injuries, and frantic families fighting for their children's well-being in a system unprepared to meet their needs.

These new systems and policies are promoting extrinsic values related to money and status at the cost of intrinsic values such as competency, authenticity, and connection. These systems and policies are about who you *should* want to be and where you *should* want to live. They do not truly respect who you are or your personal choices about your life. They do not respect an individual's right to accept and be proud of who they are and what they can do. However, it is those intrinsic values, not extrinsic, that are most highly connected to happiness. With extrinsic values at their core, the new policies being developed do not recognize real choices for individuals in supports, housing, and employment, but instead reflect the opinions and ideals of policymakers. These policies are disrespecting individuals' inherent sense of worth and undermining their basic well-being.

These policies support an individualism that we saw blossom as a result of the industrialization of our society. They support the independence that results from full employment and the perceived status of living our lives among non-disabled peers. But they are robbing individuals of a sense of capability that should not be tied to earning a specific wage and restricting their ability to make connections with like-minded, similarly abled companions.

I'm talking about giving individuals real choice and control over where and with whom they live and how they spend their days, choice and control that is not defined by federal parameters. Why should people with disabilities not be afforded the respect to choose where they find community and how they define success?

In addition, these policies often reflect unfunded mandates. Funding levels for disability services do not support the outcomes required by the accompanying rules and regulations. Also, in developing their requirements, policymakers neglected to assess or address insufficiencies in community supports, community housing, and employment opportunities. They did not invest in developing this necessary infrastructure.

The new systems are so complex and multilayered that individuals get lost among the rules and paperwork and administration of it all. The complexity has led to a pervasive lack of understanding of the system by individuals and families, which negatively impacts their ability to navigate the system, use individual budgets, and meet support needs. The layers of funding sources, varying state departments and agencies involved, and collection of case managers by many titles cannot help but lead to inefficiency and ineffectiveness.

Who is writing these rules and designing these systems? Do they have any personal or real hands-on experience with the issues that individuals with developmental disabilities or their families and caregivers deal with on a daily basis? All you have to do is talk to families or even front-line case managers to hear that they do not believe that these people do, or that they have a clear vision of what is really needed.

Yes, policy makers make an effort to include people with disabilities and their family members in advisory groups and committees. However, I can speak from experience that after serving on many committees, groups, and task forces over the years, I have seen very little family input included in final decisions about policy and design.

When families have been dealing with a myriad of intensive challenges for years, they do not need the additional challenge of a poorly designed system placing more hurdles in their paths or more responsibilities onto their already overburdened shoulders. If families could do this without help, believe me, they would. No one would choose to take on the stress, non-stop problems, and instability of dealing with public funding.

Fixing this system is going to take more than the advocacy of the limited number of voices that comprise the disability community. Most importantly, it's going to take the right people listening, the right people caring. So far, that is not happening.

For years, advocates have tried to communicate the seriousness of the worsening crisis in the direct support workforce, and prompt an appropriate response, without success. Caregivers for individuals with developmental disabilities are now called Direct Support Professionals (DSPs), reflecting the specific nature and skill level of the work that they do. But neither individuals nor providers can find enough DSPs to hire. New group homes cannot open because they can't be staffed. Supports are not developed because there are no DSPs to staff them.

DSPs provide a wide range of supports to individuals with a wide range of needs. Their work requires skill, training, and responsibility. Without them, a system of services and supports cannot exist. Yet, the average starting salary for DSPs is about $10 an hour. There needs to be a significant investment in raising pay rates and building an adequate workforce. Advocacy in some states has resulted in small increases in pay rates for DSPs, but it's not nearly enough to make a difference.

This workforce crisis is radically affecting availability and quality of care. In addition, as providers struggle to cover shifts, Medicaid rates will not pay for overtime. But providers are required by law to pay overtime. So providers must risk financial instability, cut staffing ratios, or they must hire people they would ordinarily refrain from hiring so that they are paying less overtime to competent workers. Individuals who are self-hiring staff risk uncovered shifts because they have no ability to pay overtime.

Most of the general public has no idea what the status of the disability service system is. Until you or a loved one can count yourselves among society's most vulnerable members, it's difficult to truly empathize with unwavering dependence on publicly funded supports. Before my daughter was born 30 years ago, I empathized from a comfortable distance, with arm's length compassion. With the diagnosis of Lauren's

severe disabilities, I suddenly found myself smack dab in the middle of
what I never realized was a different world, a kind of superfluous group
whose presence made people uncomfortable and defensive. It's kind of
a "there but for the grace of God go I" thankfulness coupled with "not
in my backyard" syndrome. And for many people who it hasn't touched,
it becomes just not their problem. I heard an older man once say to
someone, "Why should my tax dollars go to support your son? Take care
of your own." Oh, if only we could. This man did not see that young man
as an equal, even possibly as himself if his life had taken a different turn.
He saw him only as a non-contributing, valueless person not entitled to
more than his own family's concern and care.

As Lauren sinks deeper into her adulthood and I get closer to the end
of mine, what would it take for me to feel secure and confident that she
could survive in this world without me? In the world that I hope exists
one day, we will have...

- **AN ADEQUATELY FUNDED SYSTEM.** The disability service system
  has been perpetually underfunded. Until it is not, no amount
  of juggling or reframing of services and support mechanisms
  will be successful. Care must be taken to prevent the management and oversight of an overly complex system from eating up
  dollars more wisely spent on direct care and adequate supports
  for individuals.

- **A SYSTEM THAT IS NOT DEPENDENT ON MEDICAID.** Medicaid was originally designed as health insurance for low-income people, not to
  provide life-long community-based supports for individuals with
  developmental disabilities. Retrofitting it to do so is not working.

Because of its limitations, it cannot effectively meet the diverse, long-term needs of individuals with developmental disabilities.

- **ONE SYSTEM THAT INDIVIDUALS AND FAMILIES CAN ACCESS TO MEET ADULT AND LONG-TERM CARE NEEDS.** Funding will not need to be pieced together from various sources in order to support adult lives.

- **OR, A ONE-STOP SYSTEM.** If multiple funding sources must be tapped to bring in sufficient monies, it should not be up to individuals or families to learn about and coordinate complex funding sources. It should be the state's responsibility to create a cohesive system out of multiple parts.

- **RECOGNITION THAT ONE SIZE DOES NOT FIT ALL.** Common sense, accessibility, and flexibility will permeate a system that favors neither individuals with minimal support needs nor individuals with significant support needs.

- **A "PORTABLE" SYSTEM.** Individuals will be able to cross state lines without losing services. They can't do that now without losing supports and their place on waiting lists. Individuals will be able to join parents and siblings in other parts of the country without loss of critical services.

- **A DIRECT SUPPORT WORKFORCE THAT IS COMPENSATED COMMENSU-RATE WITH THE LEVEL OF RESPONSIBILITY AND SKILL REQUIRED TO PERFORM THEIR JOBS.** Building an adequate, well-trained work-force needs to be a priority in order for the system to function and support quality services. DSPs must be able to make a living wage.

- **STABILITY.** Without a stable and dependable service system, families cannot ever have confidence that their children will be able to survive without their oversight. Constant changes and reorganizations are a significant threat to health, safety, and general quality of life.

If the people who devise the system of services and supports are not, first and foremost, invested in that bottom line of efficient, effective, and stable, no new system or array of options will make any difference. The outcomes that individuals and their families need must drive system design, not the funding parameters and the needs of government. The lack of acceptable outcomes is evidenced by the dissatisfaction, confusion, and worry of families experiencing a lack of pervasive quality in and availability of supports.

Isn't this where the chinks in our humanity show? An affluent country like the United States should be able to provide safe and stable options for individuals with developmental disabilities and their families. But it is struggling to do so. Why? Individuals with developmental disabilities are not a priority. It's really as simple and as telling as that. Thomas Paine said, "Whether...civilization has most promoted or most injured the general happiness of man is a question that may be strongly contested. [Both] the most affluent and the most miserable of the human race are to be found in the countries that are called civilized."

I am incredibly grateful for the supports our family has received over the years. We wouldn't have survived without them. But the life my daughter is living is growing increasingly precarious. The systems that she depends on are constantly changing, and there is no guarantee that the supports she has today will continue to be there for her tomorrow. The system that provides the bulk of Lauren's support is based on Medicaid dollars and is at ever-growing risk of cuts at the federal and state levels. And, even if the system remains intact, there is no component in it to take over the management and oversight that I provide for Lauren if something should happen to me.

This instability is what scares parents to death. In fact, it is exactly why so many parents of children with disabilities will tell you, "I hope that I outlive my child." If parents would rather see their child die young than see them left in the care of this adult service system, what does that say about the system? How much fear does it take for a parent to hope for such an unnatural outcome?

After these many years of advocacy, I really cannot point to anything and say, "You know, I really made a difference there." So many of the things that I, and my fellow advocates here in New Jersey, have worked on in an attempt to build an efficient and responsive system of supports, are now no longer relevant within a totally new system. It was as if we were building not the stalwart structures we hoped would support our children for a lifetime, but rather castles of sand, vulnerable to a rising tide.

However, I can say that despite the challenges of being an advocate, I would do it all again. Along with other parent advocates—my fellow warriors—we have never let the adversity silence us. We have made it our unfaltering mission to try to build a better world for our children— a world where they can not only have dreams, but the opportunity to pursue them, and where a safe and happy life is not just our unrealized dream for them.

Made in the USA
Middletown, DE
02 December 2018